COLONEL JOHN McCORKLE.

THREE YEARS WITH QUANTRELL

A TRUE STORY

TOLD BY HIS SCOUT
JOHN McCORKLE

WRITTEN BY O. S. BARTON

ARMSTRONG HERALD PRINT
ARMSTRONG, MO.

INTRODUCTION.

In all wars there have always been, and always will be a class of men designated as guerillas, but it can be said that the Missouri guerillas are more noted than those of any war in any country for ages. Their deeds of daring, their miraculous escapes, and the physical sufferings that they endured are almost beyond belief. Following the close of the Civil War, a number of highly-colored and melodramatic books, concerning the acts of the guerillas were published, in the majority of which the desire to be sensational defeated any attempts at truthfulness on the part of the authors. Another class of books, written from an intensely partisan standpoint, has given to the world a very imperfect conception of the motives and of the conduct of the Missouri guerrillas. All of these books were published at a time when men were controlled by feelings of prejudice and passion and a number of the inhabitants of Missouri have, for years, endeavored to find someone who knew the facts and would truthfully relate them as they were.

In the summer of 1865, a tall, gaunt, blue-eyed Confederate soldier landed from a steamboat at the town of Glasgow, Howard County, Missouri. He was dressed in a ragged, faded gray uniform and had all of his possessions about him. In the country above Glasgow he had some relatives, connections, both by blood and marriage, of some of the best families in Missouri, and at the home of one of these relatives this young man found employment as a farm laborer and it soon became known that he was John McCorkle, one of Quantrell's bravest and most trusted soldiers and one of his leading scouts. For some time the neighbors kept a close watch upon the newcomer and viewed him with something of suspicion, fearing that he might follow the alleged example of some of the other of Quantrell's men and become an outlaw, but they soon found him to be a steady, law-abiding citizen. In 1867, he was married to an estimable lady of Howard County, and soon became one of its leading farmers and one of its best and most trusted citizens, and today no man in the county stands higher in the estimation of his neighbors and acquaintances than does John McCorkle. For years a member of the Baptist church, he is known as a true Christian gentleman of strong character, as tender-hearted and sympathetic as a woman, but as stern and fearless as a lion and the word "fear" has no place in John McCorkle's vocabulary. And when the time comes, he will, as he has many times in the past, face Old Death with a smile on his face.

Quite a number of his friends, knowing his history and his record with Quantrell, and knowing that from his lips would come naught but the truth, have been trying to persuade him to write a brief story of his life with Quantrell. He has at last consented and I have agreed to write the account for him. He has told me the facts and I have written them down; every word in the following pages is true: I have attempted to neither add to, or detract from any of these facts, as related by him; there is no fiction in this account but a true story. Mr. McCorkle has more than lived out his alloted time of three-score years and ten, but his memory is still good and while he may have forgotten a few of the facts after a lapse of half a century, still everything related by him actually occurred. As he would relate his experiences and those of his comrades, I could see that all the sad and awful scenes of these three terrible years were crowding fast upon his memory, and I could not help but notice the changing expression of his eyes, which are of that determined blue, while he was relating these facts to me. At times, while describing some of the battles and some of the outrages committed against the helpless non-combatants of the South, during those four yeears of civil war in Missouri by unprincipled men who hid their misdeeds under the cloak of a Federal uniform and the Stars and Stripes, I could almost see the fire flash from those eyes and at other times, while telling of the death of some comrade, or the sufferings and hardships of defenceless old men and women of the South, those same eyes would fill with tears and the voice which had so often sent terror to the hearts of Kansas Jayhawkers and militiamen as it gave forth the rebel yell, would sink into a husky whisper. This story is not published in any spirit of malice or hatred, but in order that the truth may be known, that the world may know that Quantrell and his band were justified, in nearly all of their acts and that they were not altogether bad; that they were driven to desperation by brutal outrages committed against them and their friends,

and our only desire is that the world shall know the true facts in the case before it is too late, for we all are forced to realize the sad fact that ere long "taps" will sound for the last Confederate soldier on earth. All is forgiven, if not forgotten.
O. S. Barton.

THREE YEARS WITH QUANTRELL

CHAPTER I.

I was born December 12, 1838, two miles east of Savannah, in Andrew County, Missouri, and when I was about eight years of age, my father moved from Andrew County and located on a farm near Westport, in Jackson County, Missouri. I lived with my father on this farm, attending country school in the winter time, until the year 1858, when I went to the State of Texas and stayed for six months. I then returned to my mother's farm, my father having died in 1851. I remained on the farm with my mother until April, 1861, when I, with a number of other young men, enlisted in Company A of the Missouri State Guards, near Raytown, in Jackson County. Captain Thurston was the first commander of this company. We would meet in Raytown and drill twice a week. In about a month, we were ordered to report at Independence and after remaining in Independence a short time, we were then ordered to Lock Creek and the next evening after we reached Lock Creek, we heard that Col. John P. Crittenden was coming from Kansas City with a regiment to capture us. We were then ordered to move out into the road and to form in platoons of eight. At this time, all of us, who were boys and raw recruits, became very much excited at the prospect of going into a battle and our orderly sergeant, Faulkner, became so excited that he got his saber between his knees, fell down and began to yell that the enemy were right on us. We then learned that two other companies of State Guards had come out from Independence, one called the Blues, under the command of Captain Whitehead and the other called the Grays, under the command of Captain Bob Flournoy. By this time, we had persuaded our orderly sergeant that the enemy were not on us and were ordered to join the Blues and Grays who had formed in line of battle on the hill. Col. Holloway was in command of all the State Guards. Col. Crittenden had entered the mouth of a lane about a quarter of a mile off and Col. Holloway, our commander, rode down and met him. They shook hands and after a few moments' conversation, Col. Crittenden ordered his regiment to countermarch and they turned and started back toward Kansas City. As the Federal troops marched off, Captain Whitehead, who was in command of the Blues, lost his head and ordered his company to fire and they, being as much excited as their captain, fired into our own men, wounding Col. Holloway and killing Charles Harbaugh. Colonel Holloway died in a few days at Independence from the wound.

We then returned to Independence and the next day were ordered from there to Blue Mills, east of Independence. While we were at Blue Mills, Captain Thurston and Captain Duncan of Clay County had ridden across the Little Blue on a bridge at night and as they were returning across the bridge, someone fired on them, striking Captain Duncan in the neck. He was taken from there to Doctor Twyman's at Blue Mills, where he died in a few days. After Captain Duncan was shot, Captain Thurston became very much excited, ordered us to strike our arms, disband and go home. The arms we had consisted of Burnsides rifles and sabers which had been shipped to Kansas City by the Federal Government and which we had borrowed one night from a warehouse when there was no one around. After we had gone about two miles from where we disbanded, it dawned on me that we might have further use for some of those arms and I suggested that we had better go back and get them and seven of us returned, got our rifles and sabers and a supply of ammunition and hid them in a bluff on the Little Blue. We stayed around home until after the battle of Springfield and General Price had started back to Lexington. Our company was then ordered together again and securing our guns, we marched and joined General Price at Warrensburg and came with him to Lexington and went into camp at the Fair Grounds. Before the Battle of Lexington, Captain Thurston resigned and the company elected Minor Smith, a Mexican veteran, who is still living at this time. Our company was then placed in the Seventh Missouri Regiment of Cavalry, Raines' Division and known as Rassieuer's Regiment and Lieutenant-Colonel Martin was in command. This regiment was placed on the east side of the college where the Federals were fortified, and our regiment was ordered to support the famous Bledsoe battery. For some unknown cause, Col. Rassieuer ordered our regiment to change positions and to go down a ravine and come up through the woods between the college, where the Federals were fortified and Bledsoe's Battery. General Raines who was in command took us for Federal soldiers and ordered Col. Bledsoe to open fire on us with his battery, and he fired three shots at us with his cannon, the first shot wounding seven men. When this first shot was fired, we all dropped to the ground and Col. Martin, drawing his saber in a very excited manner, ordered us to get up and stand up like men, but when Bledsoe fired the second shot, Col. Martin was the first one to fall flat on his face and John Staulcupe, a private, ran up to the Colonel and kicked him and said, "Damn you, don't be a coward; get up and stand up like a man." We then sent a runner to notify the battery of their mistake and they ceased firing on us. Our Colonel then gave the command to move fro mthere and we marched down the road under a hill where we were protected. While this battle, which lasted for three days, was in progress, one night, Henry Brookins, our First Lieutenant, proposed to me that we go up the hollow and climb a tree and look into the fort. We got permission from our Captain, but he told us positively not to fire a shot into the fort. Brookins and I went over and climbed up into two trees, where we could see into the fort. Then Brookins remarked, "John, we can't lose this chance; we must have a shot apiece," and he said "Fire." We fired and then we immediately proceeded to fall out of the trees, for a perfect hailstorm of bullets from the fort soon warned us that our elevated positions had not only been discovered, but were exceedingly dangerous. Of course, we never reported to our Captain what was the cause of the men in the fort trying to top those trees.

Immediately after the Battle of Lexington and General Mulligan had been paroled, Rassieur's Regiment was placed on guard around the fortifications, and strict orders were issued to permit no one to enter or go out of the fortifications without a pass. During this time, one of Col. Bledsoe's gunners, who was drinking very heavily, was inside the fortifications, and putting on a Federal uniform, he started to pass out. He was halted by Jim Howell, a member of my company, who demanded his pass. The gunner replied to Howell in a very insulting manner that he had no pass and was going out anyway. Howell told him what the orders were and told him to go back. The gunner kept advancing and when he started to make a rush, Howell fired and killed him. Howell regretted this fact so much that he soon resigned from the army and never entered the service again.

When General Price left Lexington, my company started South with him, but when we reached Bates County, Ike Brown and I were taken sick and left at the home of Barker Price, near Johnstown and Green Reagan was detailed to remain and take care of us. We were both suffering with what was then known as camp fever, and after remaining at Mr. Price's house for nine weeks, my younger brother, Jabez McCorkle, came down and took me back to my mother's home in Jackson County. While Brown and I were in bed at Price's, Jim Lane, the noted Kansas Redleg and murderer, came out to Mr. Price's and saw Brown and me and told us that he would be back and kill us and would give us that night to prepare to die, but for some unknown reason he did not return and I suppose the reason he did not return is that he was too busy in burning the town of Osceola and robbing and murdering its citizens. After I had been at my mother's for about a week, still being very weak from my fever, a Union man, who was a friend of our family, called on me one evening and told me that Jennison the partner and co-laborer in murdering and robbing of Jime Lane, had come within two miles of my mother's house and had murdered one of our neighbors, a very old and defenseless man, by the name of George House, and if Jennison found out that I was there he would come and murder me, although I was sick. This Union friend advised me to leave at once. That night my sister assisted me to carry my bed to a secluded spot in the woods where I stayed that night, and early the next morning, she accompanied me about eight miles to the home of our friend, John Prewitt, who hid me under a bluff on the banks of the Little Blue, where I remained for a week. His two daughters, Jane and Ellen, bringing me food and water. Remaining there for over a week, I returned to my mother's at night and there I found my brother, Jabez, who was at that time with Captain Upton Hayes, and who told me that Hayes was going south and the next morning I mounted a mule and went with him. We did not overtake Colonel Hayes and his command until we had reached Clinton in Henry County. I went with Colonel Hayes to Osceola and there I joined my old company. We stayed in camp at Osceola for about a week, and having received the news that General Fremont was attempting to cut General Price off from his march from the South, we were ordered to Springfield on a forced march.

CHAPTER II.

On the second morning after leaving Osceola when I awoke I found that I was too sick to proceed with the army, who broke camp very early in the morning and was left to follow later. I stayed in the camp alone until about noon, when I realized the danger I was in and, weak as I was, I mounted and started to follow the army. I managed to ride until about dark when I stopped at a farmer's house and asked if I might stay all night. He told me that he was perfectly willing to keep me, but was afraid that the Federals would capture me and kill me as there were a great many Federal militia in that country. I told him that I would die from weakness if I attempted to go farther that night, and he consented that I might remain. The next morning, I left his house early in the morning and reached Springfield late the next night. It seemed that Fate was against my proceeding south with Price for after being in camp at Springfield for ten days, the measles broke out among the soldiers and I was detailed to take charge of seven of the boys, my brother, Jabez, being among the number, and take them to a house about three miles from Springfield and nurse them through their sickness. I was isolated from the rest of the army and in about a week, some of the boys having grown worse, I saddled my horse with the intention of riding to Springfield to consult with a physician and to procure medicines and provisions for the sick men. I had ridden only a short distance when I met the physician who asked me where I was going, and informed me that there were no more Confederates in Springfield, that they had started South and General Fremont was in possession of the town. The physician advised me to take a flag of truce and go to Springfield and surrender myself and my seven sick men. This I refused to do. He then asked me to accompany him to another house where there were some sick soldiers, where we were detained for about an hour and I left the physican there and started back to see my sick boys. Imagine my consternation when upon reaching the house I found it deserted, a squad of Federals having been there during my absence and taken all the boys back to Springfield as prisoners. I then started south and riding a few miles I stopped at a house, hitched my horse to the stile-blocks and as I started through the yard to the front door, a lady came running out of the side-door and told me that there were some Federal soldiers in the house and unless I wanted to be captured I had better be moving away. Not waiting for any further orders, I wheeled and started on the run and, placing my hands upon the top plank of the fence, I put spurs to my horse and dashed away. I soon came to a little prairie and looking back, I saw a company of Federals coming after me. I immediately increased my speed and reached the woods ahead of them and turned abruptly south until I reached Wilson Creek at a point where there was a water-mill. The mill was running, but no one was there. I noticed a house up on the hill west of the mill and saw three or four men standing in the yard, and as I rode up to them, I noticed that one of the men had an old Mississippi rifle in his hand and I, of course, took them to be some of Price's men. I asked them to direct me to the road over which Price's army had gone; one of them directed me, but as I started to ride through the gate, another man caught my horse by the bridle and the man with the Mississippi rifle presented it at my breast, remarking that they would take care of me and take me back to Springfield. My pistol being empty, I immediately obeyed and dismounted. They took me into the house with them, where we had a good supper and, after supper one of them brought out a basket of apples and we all sat around until a late hour discussing the war and its probable end. I was then shown to my room, which was to be occupied with me by the owner of the Mississippi rifle. I still had my pistol buckled around me, and as I went to undress, I threw it on the bed, remarking, "That pistol is empty: if it had been loaded, you might have had a little fun in taking me." The owner of the rifle broke into a hearty laugh and remarked, "Well, the rifle that I captured you with was empty too." the next morning, the owner of the place, who had been out somewhere all night, came home, accompanied by two other men, one of them had the longest and largest shot-gun I ever saw. It looked to me as if the barrels were at least ten feet long and I thought they had sent out in the night and procured it for the express purpose of shooting me with. We then started back to Springfield and after we had crossed Wilson Creek near the mill, my captors left the main road, turning up a bridle path through a ravine. I could hardly ride for thinking that they were taking me into the woods to shoot me and I kept my eyes constantly on the gentleman with the big gun; but in a short time, we reached the road that Price had taken in his march south. About this time, we met the entire command of Federals going south, following Price, and I was taken along with them. They had with them sixteen other Confederates, including Colonel Freeman and forage master. After proceeding a short distance, we met a man in citizen's clothes, who told us that Price was about four miles south of us in camp. The regiment to which I was turned over was the Seventh Missouri Cavalry, and leaving the prisoners with a guard, moved forward after Price. In a short time, we heard four cannon shots, one of the guards remarking, "Just listen to that: they are giving old Price Hell now; they're going to eat him up." The cannonading at first sounded like distant thunder, approaching nearer and nearer, and in less than an hour, the federal cavalry came into sight, rushing at break-neck speed through the brush and ordered guards and prisoners to mount and retreat to Sprinfield on the double quick. Some of our boys then remarked to the guard, "You were mistaken about who was catching hell, wasn't you?" While we were riding back toward Springfield, a Federal private rode out of line and coming up to us Confederate prisoners, drawing his revolver, began to flourish it and curse, and said, "You damned rebels I ought to shooe every one of you." Along the road in that section there were a great many abandoned shafts of lead and zinc mines, and just about the time that this gallant and brave soldier had worked himself into a frenzy, he and his horse both suddenly disappeared through a brush pile, having gone into a hidden shaft, but, unfortunately, the man was not much hurt, although his horse was killed; and the next morning he was called before his colonel, who gave him a severe reprimand, took his side-arms away from him and ordered him to report to the infantry, telling him that may be service in infantry would teach him to treat prisoners with respect. We were then taken back to the headquarters of the commander, where a description was taken of us, and our horses taken from us and we were started back to Springfield afoot. The seventeen prisoners were placed under charge of a lieutenant with twenty-seven guards and we started back to walk the twenty-seven miles to Springfield. This lieutenant and his men treated us all with courtesy, the lieutenant going ahead and securing provisions for us, waiting on the roadside with a large basket well filled with provisions. Upon reaching Springfield the prisoners were placed under guard in the third story of a brick building. The next morning, while sitting in this room with the other boys, I noticed a Union soldier who kept watching me very closely. Whenever I would turn my head, he would change his position, so as to see my face, his conduct made me nervous. I got up and went to the window and, leaning out, was looking down upon the street. He left the room, went down to the street and looked up into my face again. I returned to my seat in the room; he came back, walked up to me, put his hand on my shoulder and remarked, "Is not your name McCorkle?" I replied in the affirmative and he told me that his name was Frank Hoerheimer, that he had known me in Newton County, where I had been at his father's house and attended a number of dances with him. I was very anxious to go to the hospital to see how my brother and the other sick boys were and Frank went to Colonel Mills, who was in command there, and told the Colonel that if he would let me go to the hospital to see the sick boys, he would go with me and be responsible. We went over and my brother, Jabez and I went out in town and took dinner with Frank. When I first went into the hospital, one of the boys whom I had nursed, George Shue, by name, took me by the hand and said, "John, I am awful sick; I feel very queer. Please tell the doctor to come." I went upstairs where the physician was and, after some little time, succeeded in finding him and took him down to see Shue, but when we reached George's cot, the poor fellow had gone to that land where there is no fighting. I then went to Frank Hoerheimer and Lieutenant Baker and made arrangements for his burial and his dust today sleeps in the graveyard at Springfield.

Soon after we had reached Springfield, as prisoners, Lieutenant Baker tried to persuade my brother and me to take the oath of allegiance and return home, and one night he came to me and told me that on the next day we would be removed to St. Louis and there placed in prison, and that we would have to travel eighty miles by foot to Rolla. After consulting with my brother and other friends, and having come to the conclusion that Fate was against my ever reaching Price's army, brother and I took the oath of allegiance, were given our paroles and started back to Jackson County, Missouri, afoot. Brother was still very weak and our progress was, of necessity, very slow. I carried all the baggage we had, which consisted of a cheap suit of clothes each, two blankets, one of them a fine Mexican overcoat blanket, which were packed in an old-fashioned carpet bag. While in prison in Springfield, brother and I both had acquired thousands of those little friends of the soldier, that sticketh closer than a brother, familiarly known as "gray-backs," and these friends of ours entertained us along our weary tramp and kept us from sleeping too soundly at night. After we had reached Cedar County, we saw a man and woman coming toward us in a wagon and upon their approach we recognized a friend of ours from Jackson County, Missouri, by the name of William Fox, the lady with him being his wife. Fox was glad to see us and directed us to go on to his house and stop. After leaving Fox we met another old gentleman, whom we had known before in Jackson County, but who had fallen from grace and become a strong Union man and, with all of our talking, we could not persuade him that he had ever seen us or heard of us before, but he gave us some very fatherly advice, to the effect that if we had any preparations to make for the future, we had better be making them, for no rebel could live in that county. After leaving our unfriendly friend, we met another marauder garbed in a Federal uniform, in the person of a young man with a large rifle. He presented the rifle and halted us, asking us where we were from and demanding our passports, which we showed him and of which I am satisfied he could not read a word. He then demanded to search our baggage, which he did and then proceeded with us to Fox's house, where he again wanted to search our baggage, telling us that if we would give him the Mexican blanket, he would bother us no more. We decided to give it to him and in less than an hour he came back with another man who was armed with a shotgun and walking up to me the latter placed the muzzle of the gun to my breast and said, "Damn you! surrender." I told him we had already surrendered and taken the oath. He lowered his gun and the two of them took all of our clothing and two dollars and a half, being all the money we had. When our friend Fox returned home, we related to him our experience with these two brave Union soldiers and he reported the fact to the Lieutenant who was in command of the home guards and he and Fox tried to recover our property for us, but only succeeded in recovering the Mexican blanket, which these two thieves dropped in their flight. The next morning Fox accompanied us about twelve miles, letting my brother ride his horse and he walked with me. He told us to avoid the town of Humansville, in Polk County, because there was a company of militia there, who were a hard set. Leaving this town about two miles to our right, we walked on till sundown, and, seeing a man in his barn-lot, feeding his stock, I asked permission to stay all night, frankly telling him who we were and the feeble condition of my brother. He said that he had just returned from Bolivar, where he had taken an oath not to aid, abet or protect any Southern soldier, under penalty of death, and then added, "But boys, I am a Southern man and love the South, and if you are willing to risk staying with me I will risk it, and if they come and find you here, they can do no more than kill us and we'll all die together, but we will try to take some of the blue-coated devils with us, as I have some guns hidden." We went into his house, his wife prepared us a nice supper, and when he suggested it was time to retire, I told him about our traveling companions, the graybacks, and that we did not want to infect his beds. He replied, "That makes no difference; I am a Southern man, and nothing I have is too good for a Southern soldier. The beds can be cleaned." This statement made us feel better, of course. We left early the next morning, and having been fortunate enough to ride in a wagon part of the way, we reached the place where the town of Osceola had once been, but there was no town there, as General Jim Lane, of Kansas, had shortly before made it a visit and, following his universal practice, had left only ashes. Here I sold the Mexican blanket for five dollars. Just after we had crossed the Osage River, we met Tom Carter and a man by the name of Younger, a cousinn of Cole's, and went to Carter's house and stayed until the next day. From there we went to Lone Jack, where we met John Little, Sam Montgomery and Dick Hopkins, who belonged to Colonel Quantrell's command. After leaving Lone Jack, we went to my uncle, John Wigginton's, who lived fourteen miles south of Independence. We stayed with Uncle John until the next day, when my brother and I went on to our mother's home, where we received a tearful and hearty welcome. There we changed our clothes and parted company with our traveling companions, the graybacks. In a few days, it was decided that my brother would stay with my mother and try to raise a crop and I went down to Uncle John Wigginton's and intended to farm there with him on shares. This was in the spring of 1862.

CHAPTER III.

I fully intended, when I started in to raise this crop with my uncle, to remain a quiet, law-abiding citizen. I had taken the oath of allegiance at Springfield and had been given a passport, showing to the world that I was a law-abiding American citizen and still entitled to protection under the law, but before the ink was hardly dry on that passport, I had been robbed of all I had, and that by men who claimed to be in the service of the United States government. I tried to forget these outrages and work on the farm, but before I had gotten my crop planted, a squad of Federal soldiers came by and compelled me twice a week to accompany them with a mail carrier twelve or fifteen miles and then to walk back, claiming that prior to this time, some Southern men had fired on the mail carrier and I would be a protection to him. Not satisfied with taking me from my crop two or three days out of each week, in July, one Lieutenant Swann, who hailed from that loyal state of Kansas and who had been in command of the mail-carrier's bodyguard, notified me that I must appear at Independence before Captain Mayhew, the Provost-Marshal. I obeyed, and when I presented myself to Captain Mayhew, he told me he knew of no charges against me, but to present myself in person to the commander, Colonel Buell. I asked Colonel Buell what charges were preferred against me, and, in a very gruff, insulting manner, he told me he had heard of my conduct and for me to return to the Provost-Marshal and give a bond of $5,000 for my good behavior. I then asked Colonel Buell what I had been doing and the only charge that he could remember against me was that I had been singing some rebel songs. This offense, if offense it was, was true for on one occasion, in going from my uncle's to my mother's I was singing that song, two lines of which are:

We'll hang John Brown on a sour apple tree
And feed Jeff Davis on peaches and cream,
and, while singing this song, I had passed Alfred Lee's house, where ten or twelve Federal soldiers were quartered. They ran out into the road, halted me and took me back to the house of my uncle, John Fristoe, where their captain was an unwelcome guest. They kept me there all night with them, having me to again sing about John Brown and other

COLONEL WILLIAM QUANTRELL.

22b

rebel songs. The next morning, hearing them cursing, firing their pistols in the yard and saying "some damned bushwhacker had stolen one of their halters," I started down where they were, when Dan Davidson, a stage driver, who was staying at my uncle's, told me not to go, that they would shoot me. I told him I reckoned not, that I had been given protection by the government, and he said that protection, passports nor anything else from the Federal government made any difference to that bunch. I stayed upstairs until after they had gone and then went back to my uncle's where I was living. One Saturday afternoon, my cousin, George Wigginton, and I went over to Big Cedar Church, where there was a singing school. While we were in the church, a company of Federals rode up and examined every saddle, looking for gun marks. When we returned from the singing school, Mollie Wigginton told us that there had been a company of Federal soldiers there that evening, leaving an order for George and me to come to Independence the next Monday and to enlist in the State Militia, and that unless we did report, that they would come back and take Mollie and put her in prison and hold her until we did report. Now imagine, if you can, my feelings. I honestly and conscientiously believed in the principles of the Confederacy, had started out to fight, and, if necessary, to give my life for those principles, but, on account of sickness and misfortune, had been captured, and, that I might save my brother and myself from languishing and dying in a Federal dungeon, I had taken the oath of allegiance to the Federal government with the full intention of abiding by it; I had returned to Jackson County, Missouri, where my mother and all my relatives were living, had gone to work, trying to be a peaceable, law-abiding citizen, but I had been constantly harrassed, annoyed and threatened, had been forced to leave my farm and my crops twice a week; I had been required to give a bond of Five Thousand dollars for merely singing a foolish song, and now, under the penalty of having a pure, innocent girl, my cousin, Mollie Wigginton, imprisoned in a Northern dungeon, to probably meet a fate far more terrible than death itself; after all this I was ordered to enlist in an alien army and to take up arms against the cause I loved and against my own people. I could not and I would not longer submit, and I then resolved that if die I must, I would die fighting for my own people and for their cause, so, when George Wigginton asked me what I intended to do, I promptly told him that I was going to find Colonel Quantrell's command and join it whereupon, he replied with equal promptness, "John, I am going with you."

CHAPTER IV.

After the execution, in Virginia, of the famous abolitionist, John Brown, a number of men who had been with him in his attempt to make Kansas a free state, organized, at the town of Lawrence, a company of free lances, who were familiarly called the Kansas Redlegs. The leaders of this band were General Jim Lane and Colonel Jennison, names which became watchwords of terror to the inhabitants of the border counties of Missouri.

During the Pike's Peak excitement, a young man, by the name of William Clark Quantrell, left his home in Maryland, accompanied by his younger brother, a boy of eighteen years, and taking with them two negro men they started west for the Pike's Peak Country. When they reached Jackson County, Missouri, they supplied themselves with two wagons and two four-mule teams. After laying in a quantity of supplies, these two boys, with their two negroes acting as drivers, left Missouri and started for Colorado. On the first night out, they camped ten or twelve miles south of Fort Leavenworth, Kansas, and, thinking that they were in a civilized country, were soon asleep. About midnight, thirty of the Kansas Redlegs rode up to the camp and, without any warning, fired a volley into the two sleeping boys, killing the younger brother and breaking the thigh of William Quantrell. These *loyal* citizens then appropriated to their own use the eight head of mules, the wagons and all provisions and, taking the two negroes with them, left the two boys, they supposed to be dead on the plains of Kansas. When daylight came, William Quantrell crawled to the lifeless body of his brother and, after discovering that his young life had passed out, he crawled around, pulling up the grass, and covered up the dead body. Being unable to walk a step, he started to crawl across the prairie, hoping to find aid. He crawled until nearly noon, when an Indian found him, and having more heart and sympathy than the white men of Kansas, the Indian tenderly placed the wounded boy on his saddle and, getting behind him, took him to Fort Leavenworth. He was taken to the hospital there and, in several months, partially recovered the use of his limb. His money and property all having been taken from him, he sought and secured employment ne arL eavenworth, Kansas, as a school teacher, where he taught during the coming wniter. In the spring, he went to California and again engaged in school teaching. All the time he was teaching, he was known as the Melancholy Teacher. Constantly brooding over the fate of his brother and the way he had been treated, when his term of school ended in California, he decided to return to Kansas, and, if possible, find the perpetrators of this outrage and to be revenged. He returned to Fort Leavenworth, and staying there only a few weeks, he went to Lawrence, Kansas, going under the name of Charles Hart. In a short time, he learned who the leaders of the Redlegs were, and becoming well acquainted with Jim Lane and Jennison, he joined their band and would accompany them on their horse stealing raids in the border counties of Kansas. He soon learned who the men were that had murdered his brother and robbed him, and on every raid that he would make with these men, from one to three of the men he had spotted would fail to return and would afterwards be found with a bullet hole in the forehead. His greatest desire was to kill the leader of this band of thirty, and with this end in view, he accompanied six of this band in a raid that they had planned into Jackson County, Missouri, to steal some negroes from a man by the name of Walker, who was a large slave holder. The plan these gentlemen worked was to go into Missouri, forcibly take slaves into Kansas and hide them and when the Missouri owners would offer rewards for them, they would return the slaves, secure the reward, take several horses and cattle with them and return to Kansas, and, in a few weeks, return, steal the negroes again and collect another reward. When they had reached Walker's home, Quantrell went into the house and told Walker's son, Mr. Walker being absent from home, what they had intended to do, and told him that when they had entered the house to take the negroes, that he, Quantrell, would shoot the leader of the Redlegs. Just as they entered the house, Mr. Walker, who had returned, stepped in. The leader demanded his money and four negroes. Quantrell drew his revolver, but, before he could fire, Mr. Walker, not understanding his object, struck the pistol and he missed the leader. The Kansans hurriedly left, two of them hiding on a creek back of Mr. Walker's house, where they were found the next day by Quantrell, Mr. Walker and his son. Quantrell commanded them to surrender and received a reply from one of them, "Take that, you damned traitor," accompanied by a shot which went wild and was answered by shots from Quantrell and Walker and there were two less Kansas Redlegs. Quantrell remained in Missouri, assisting the citizens in defending their property and in catching these horse, cattle and negro thieves, and occasionally paying a debt he owed the Redlegs who had killed his brother. In 1861, after the war had started, Quantrell had six men with him, who were assisting in a search for these Jayhawkers, and thought he was assisting the Federal troops in preventing these outrages. On two different occasions, while Quantrell was out with his men, he was fired upon by a company of Federal soldiers and got away from them without returning the fire. He then went into Independence and told the authorities that he was trying to assist them in putting down this lawlessness and that he was also getting tired of the Federal soldiers firing on him and his men and that he would not run from them any more. In a short time, about ten or twelve Federal soldiers fired onto him and his men and they very promptly returned the fire, killing five of the soldiers and chasing the remainder into Independence. From that time on, the Federal soldiers and the Kansas Jayhawkers devoted a great deal of time and energy in attempting to catch Quantrell and his men.

On the night after we had received the order to to come to Independence and enlist, George Wigginton and I mounted our horses and started to find Quantrell. eW first went to the home of Dave Tally, Quantrell. We went first to the home of Dave Tally, who directed us to Cole Younger's camp in the brother, Jabez McCorkle, Dick Tally, Tom Tally, Jim Morris and Tom Rice. When we had told Cole Younger our object, he asked us what arms we could get and I secured a rifle and eight cartridges and George a double-barreled shot-gun. We remained in camp in the woods until the next Saturday when we received word to join Quantrell Sunday night at Blue Springs. On Sunday morning the eight of us met at Uncle John Wigginton's where they had prepared for us an elegant dinner and, immediately after dinner, we bid them good-bye and left. When we arrived at Blue Springs, we found that Quantrell, who had been joined by Colonel Upton Hayes, Colonel Hughes and Colonel Thompson, had left word for us to meet them at the bridge crossing the Little Blue near Independence. When we reached the bridge, Quantrell selected all the men who had revolvers and Cole Younger, Tom Tally and Jim Morris were among this number. When we prepared to leave, Quantrell had sixty men, and Colonel Hughes assumed command of the remainder, amounting to about 350, raw recruits, old soldiers and boys. It was agreed between the two officers that Quantrell was to dash through Independence, direct to the camp of the Federals on the Kansas City road and Colonel Hughes was to follow him through, not stopping in the town because the Federals were fortified in the court-house and a bank building, where Colonel Buell had his headquarters. Just at day-break on the tenth day of August, 1862, Colonel Quantrell rode out before his sixty men and, saying "Come on, boys," dashed through the town of Independence, followed by Colonel Hughes and his command. When we reached the court-house square, Colonel Hughes ordered us to dismount and he sprang over the fence into the court-house yard and immediately the Federals opened fire on us from the court-house and bank building. Colonel Hughes and Colonel

Thompson were both wounded at the first volley. Colonel Hayes took command then and ordered us to go at double quick to the camp of the Federals. As we came in sight of the camp, the Federals were running, trying to get behind some rock fences, most of them, having failed to stop to put on their clothes, but many of them carrying their guns. As soon as we reached the Federal camp, I ran into a tent and found a box of ammunition. I pitched it out and told the boys to help themselves and filled my cartridge box. About this time, Colonel Hayes noticed some of the Federal soldiers behind the rock fence on the Kansas City road and, calling me to him, said "John, you are the only man with a long-range rifle. Make those fellows take their heads down." I fired, but the first shot fell short. I fired the second shot and they all fell off the fence and didn't stick their heads up any more. Most of the Federal troops had gotten behind the rock fence on a hill towards the town of Independence and, north of this rock fence, there was a hedge fence, an orchard and a sweet potato patch. Colonel Hayes called for volunteers to go behind the hedge and rout them from behind the rock fence. One of our bravest men, Barney Chambers, a Presbyterian minister, volunteered to lead us and thirty of us accompanied him and got behind the hedge fence. Chambers gave the order to fire and the enemy returned our fire with a perfect hailstorm of minie balls that literally mowed the hedge fence from over our heads. Poor Chambers was killed, being the only man struck. The Federals continued their fire, when we decided to retreat. In my haste to get away, I stumbled and fell between two sweet potato rows and my brother Jabez hid behind an apple tree. There were at least twenty-five balls struck the tree he was behind and the balls threw the dust and dirt over me until I was in danger of being buried alive. When they had ceased firing at us, Brother asked me if I was wounded, and, telling him no, I started for a tree, the Federals opening fire on us again. We remained behind these trees a few moments, exchanging shots with the Federals when we suddenly discovered that he and I were the only ones on our side in sight, and we immediately retreated in great haste over the brow of the hill. While we were running away, my cousin, George Wigginton, received a wound in the thigh and Rice was wounded in the instep. Colonel Hayes told me that he was afraid that we would have to retreat and for me to make some provisions to take the two boys away with us for he was satisfied that if the Federals captured them they would be killed. I went down to an old mill and secured an old delivery wagon and a horse, but when I went to harness the horse, I found there were no lines. The miller's wife came to the door and told me to take her clothes line and use it for lines. I then started to assist the boys into the wagon when she ran out of the house and told me that I could not put those boys into that wagon, and, running back into the house, she returned with a feather bed and throwing it into the wagon, she remarked "Now, put 'em in." During this time, Quantrell, who had been pursuing the Federals toward Kansas City returned and, dashing up into the town, began to fire at the windows of the court house and bank building. Discovering that he was unable to dislodge the Federals, called for volunteers to rush in and set fire to the bank building. Cole Younger and my brother volunteered, and, rushing to a nearby carpenter shop, they gathered an armful of shavings each, Cole going to the front door, and my brother to the rear door, and, piling the shavings against the doors, set fire to them. The men, in the meantime, kept a constant fire at the windows. As soon as the smoke began to rise, the Federals ran out a white flag and said they would surrender if they would be treated as prisoners of war, afterwards saying that they would have surrendered before, but knowing it was Quantrell and his men, they were afraid. They were assured that they would be treated as prisoners of war and were drawn up in line on the courthouse square and disarmed and were paroled and let go free.

When we first entered Independence, there were confined in the county jail two Southern men, Frank Harbaugh and Bill Bassham, who had been sentenced by the Federal officers to be shot the next day. Neither of these men had ever taken any part in the war, Harbaugh being a farmer and Bassham in the employ of the Government, carrying the overland mail. As soon as we had entered the town, George Todd took ten men with him and went to the jail and, securing sledge hammers from a blacksmith shop, broke the doors in and released these two men. As soon as they were free, Bassham began calling for a gun and was told to go to the provost-marshal's office, which was filled with guns that had been taken from the Southern citizens. He rushed to the office, secured him a double-barrelled shot gun, and immediately began to try to get even with the men that had put him in jail, but Harbaugh didn't seem to desire any gun, but started for home on a dead run and I have never seen nor heard of him since, but suppose he has stopped running ere this. Among the men captured by us was a neighbor boy of mine, Anderson Cowgill, whom I had known for years and after he was paroled, I went up to him and offered to speak to him, but he refused, saying, "I will get even with you yet," and how well he kept his word will appear later in these pages.

We then destroyed all of the Federal camps and, taking all their guns, ammunition and supplies that we could carry, we left Independence and went into camp on Morgan Rucker's farm near Blue Springs, where we remained until the morning of the eleventh of August, where Quantrell reorganized his company consisting of 120 men and we were all sworn into the Confederate service by Colonel Thompson, who was at that time still suffering from the wound he had received at Independence. The next day word was brought that Colonel Hoyt with his Kansas Redlegs was on the east side of East Blue, burning the houses of Southern people. Colonel Thompson assumed command and we started in pursuit of Hoyt, aiming to intercept him at Hickory Grove, but he had passed before we had reached there and was so far ahead that we were unable to overtake him, and he returned to the State of Kansas. Here we separated from Thompson and Hayes, they going to Lone Jack, where, on the next day, the hardest fought battle, considering the number on each side, was fought. After leaving Hayes and Thompsonn, word was brought to Quantrell that Hoyt was returnning to burn the town of Independence. He immediately divided into two groups of sixty men each, he taking one group to Independence and the other groups, under the command of William Haller, went over on the Sni. When we reached Independence, Jim Stevenson and I were detailed as pickets on the road leading from Kansas City to Independence. We stayed there all that night, the orderly sergeant having forgotten us, and the next afternoon, two pickets came out from Haller's groups and informed us that Quantrell had left Independence during the previous night. We camped there until the next day and Colonel Quantrell having returned, we left for Lone Jack, where we found the commands of Colonel Hayes, Colonel Vard Cockrell, Colonel Coffey and Colonel Thompson, they having succeeded in finally whipping the Federals after a hard fight. We learned that among the Federals captured there was a certain Lieutenant, Levi Copeland, from the state of Kansas, who had been making himself exceedingly obnoxious to the Southern people of Jackson county, who had a short time before gone to the house of a very old man, who had two sons in our company, and having demanded of the father the surrender of his two boys and being told that he knew nothing of their whereabouts, Copeland and his men took him to a tree within a few feet of his front porch and

COLE YOUNGER.

34b

there, in the presence of his wife and daughters, hanged him, remarking as he rode off. "This is what I do to all damned rebel sympathizers." When Quantrell learned that Copeland was a prisoner under charge of Colonel Coffey, he wrote a note, demanding that Copeland be turned over to him. Coffey replied that he could not do it. Quantrell immediately wrote him another note, telling him fully what Copeland had done and also telling him that unless Copeland was turned over to him by a certain hour, that he would take his company and charge Coffey's command and take Copeland by force, and just before the time was up, Quantrell gave us the command to saddle and mount, and, just at that time, two men appeared and turned Copeland over to us. Quantrell questioned him, then called for the two sons of the old man he hung, remarking, "Boys, he's yours." The two boys led him a short distance into the woods and the reports of two pistols soon told the end of Levi Copeland.

We remained in camp at Lone Jack several days and going down near Bone Hill, justs as we were getting ready to eat breakfast, our pickets informed us that there was a regiment of militia from Lexington rapidly approaching. We immediately mounted and rode about ten miles up the Sni and started to cross the prairie to Blue Springs and when in about a mile of Blue Springs, we met a man who told us that there was another regiment of Federals coming from Blue Springs after us. We turned to the South, crossed the Sni and, as we started up the bottom, we ran almost into Jennison's Kansas regiment, engaged in their usual pastime of burning houses. Quantrell gave the command to counter-march. We then re-crossed the Sni and started across the six-mile prairie to Big Creek. As we entered the prairie, Cole Younger was detaild to fall back with twenty men and act as rear guard to Quantrell's force. When we had gotten about half way across the prairie Younger sent to Quantrell for reinforcements, as the Federals were pressing us hard. Quantrell sent word to cross over to a nearby ridge, where he would form a battle line and give battle to the Federals. We dashed for the ridge and just as we got there Quantrell came up, with the Federals in close pursuit. They did not see us until they were less than thirty yards distant when, yelling and firing our guns, we charged them. They lost nine men, while we lost only one.

After this skirmish we marched to Big Creek, crossed it and went about three miles up the creek. The next morning we started across the prairie to the head of the Little Blue. When we had gone about five miles down the Little Blue we discovered that a large force of Federals were on our trail, and that they outnumbered us ten to one. We then crossed the prairie, riding swiftly to avoid the pursuing Federals. Suddenly we came upon another force of encamped in a pasture. We dashed by them before they could make an attack. Finally we came to a bridge across the Blue, and we destroyed the bridge and put an end to further pursuit. After traveling for several days we came in the neighborhood of Lone Jack. There we encountered a regiment of

Federals. We struck back towards the Blue and the next day decidd to disband as Federal troops were scattered over the whole country.

Ike Bassham and I started out together. We came to a house where a man by the name of Cummins lived. We went into the house to see if we could get some breakfast.

While we were waiting for breakfast, we heard the front gate open and close and, looking out of the window, we saw the Federal lieutenant and an orderly sergeant walking toward the house. We sprang to the door with a revolver in each hand, when the lieutenant, who was in front, threw up his hands and said, "If you won't shoot, I won't," to which Bassham replied, "Then get out of this yard, and damned quick." They wheeled and started to the gate, the orderly sergeant going through the gate, but the lieutenant in his hurry missed it, and bolted right through the hedge fence, leaving his coat tail and a good deal of his blue uniform hanging on the thorns. Just then a negro came around the house and told us that there was a company of Federals camped about a quarter of a mile from the house and were simply separated, hunting their breakfast. Bassham and I immediately decided that we were not hungry, and bidding Mr. Cunningham a hasty good morning and apologizing for leaving before breakfast, we rushed out, interrupted our horses in the midst of their breakfast, sprung into our saddles and rushed into the woods. After riding about five miles, we stopped at the Widow Dillingham's and our appetites having returned, we ate a hearty breakfast. While we were waiting to go South, it was reported to Colonel Quantrell that two men who had been with him, Carlyle and Black, had been taking horses from farmers and telling that Quantrell had ordered them to take them, and that they would then take the horses to Lexington and sell them for a high price. Six other men with myself were sent out to look for them. We captured them and brought them to Quantrell, together with eight horses that they had stolen. Quantrell made them return the horses to their owners and told them that if they were guilty of this again, he would have them shot. They stayed in camp for a week or two, when the citizens again came to Colonel Quantrell and asked him what he wanted with so many horses and told him that these men were still stealing horses. He then took ten of us with him and found Carlyle at his brother-in-law's, a man by the name of Thompson. We knocked on the door and, being admitted into Thompson's bedroom, we found his bed empty, but Will Hulse finally discovered him on a trundle bed beneath the other bed. Quantrell told Hulse to throw back the top mattress and he would just shoot him through the straw tick. Carlyle immediately jumped out, turning the bed over. The colonel then compelled him to tell where the horses he had been stealing were and he took us to their hiding place in the dense woods where we discovered sixteen head of horses that he had stolen. Carlyle was placed on a horse and a rope tied around his neck, and the horse was led from under him. The next day the horses were returned to their owners.

Shortly after this, sixteen of us, under the command of Colonel Quantrell stopped at the house of a man by the name of Tate, four miles south of Westport, where we stopped, intending to stay all night. This house was two stories in front, with a one-story ell in the rear. It was built of logs, but afterwards weatherboarded. A picket was placed in the road. Being very tired we all retired early and were soon asleep, Colonel Quantrell and Cole Younger occupying the bed and the remainder of us sleeping on the floor. About midnight it began to rain very hard and it was exceedingly dark. About one o'clock, our picket dashed by the house, firing his pistol and calling to us to get out as we were surrounded by Federals and we soon found that about four hundred had surrounded the house. Not knowing that the house was built of logs, the Federals began to fire into the walls, calling on us to surrender. One of our boys called to them to cease firing until Mr. Tate and his family could get out of danger, which they did. When Tate and his family had gotten out of the house, an officer came to the door and tried to open it, calling on us to surrender. Quantrell, who was sitting on the bed, said, "Boys, get away from that door a minute." He then fired his pistol through the door and the Federal officer fell, mortally wounded. Another officer ran up and we heard him say, "Boys, he's dead. I'll go to the door and make them surrender," and as soon as he rattled the door, Quantrell fired again and he fell, mortally wounded. At this time, one of our men began to beg us to surrender and said he wanted to surrender. Quantrell called to the Federals to cease firing a few minutes, that he had a "damned coward" in there that he wanted to give to them. They ceased firing and we put our coward out of the window.

All this time, we could hear the officers on the outside telling their men to shoot low, that we were lying on the floor, but their bullets had no effect on the heavy weatherboarding and logs. We then discovered that they had set fire to the house and that they had withdrawn a short distance from the house, waiting for us to emerge. Quantrell went upstairs, and stepping out of a window onto the roof of the ell part of the house, fired at the commander, with a double-barrelled shot gun, killing him instantly. While he was upstairs some of the boys found a door leading out into the back yard and told Quantrell of it. Quantrell said, "As they have set fire to the house this door will be our only means of safety; some of us are bound to be killed. Now I will go first, you boys follow me; stoop and jump as far as you can, shooting with both hands.' The Federals were drawn on either side of the door. Quantrell opened the door, shooting the Federal who was standing near it and we all sprang after him, shooting with both hands. The Federals opened fire on us from both sides, killing their own men. We ran into the garden, through a gooseberry patch and through the garden fence, literally tearing the fence down and then out into a stalk field and then into the timber. The only wounds any of us had were made by the thorns of the gooseberry bushes. Cole Younger suffered more from the gooseberry bushes than any of us, having run out of the house without his boots and we teased him a good deal about the Federals running him out of his boots. We learned from the neighbors afterwards that there were over forty Federals killed, but most of them were killed by their own fire when they were attempting to cross-fire us as they escaped.

One day, shortly after this, Cole Younger and I decided to go out and see if we could locate the Federals. We passed Sam Caldwell's house and Mrs. Caldwell and her sister came out and stood on the stile-blocks and talked to us a while. We left them and started down the road. We had gone about a quarter of a mile, we turned into a lane, and, to our utter surprise, were face to face with about eighty Federals. They commanded us to halt, which we answered with pistol shots and, wheeling our horses, we started back in the direction of Caldwell's house, followed by the Federals, shooting at us, constantly, and, to our consternation, we saw the two women standing on the stile blocks watching us. Cole Younger yelled to them to lie down, which they did behind the blocks and, as we dashed by them, with the Federals in close pursuit, still keeping up a constant fire at us, they called to us, "Run, boys, run, and lay low on your horses." By this time, we had gone over the brow of the hill and turned into the woods and the Federals gave up the chase. The only damage they did to us was to shoot part of Cole Younger's stirrup off.

CHAPTER VI.

Late in the fall of 1862, 140 of us, consisting of a few new men and Quantrell's original company, met at Lone Jack and started south. When we had reached a point on the road in Cass County, between Harrisonville and Dayton, we discovered a provision train of fourteen wagons, guarded by a company of Federal soldiers. Colonel Quantrell commanded us to charge them and, after firing only a few shots, they scattered in different directions and here was where I captured my first Federal soldier. I pursued him for about a quarter of a mile and when he discovered that I was gaining on him, he stopped his horse, threw up his hands and asked me not to shoot him. I told him to hand me his rifle, which he did, and taking the cap off of it, I handed it back to him and demanded his revolver. When he handed me his belt, there was no revovler in the scabbard. He had dropped it in his flight. I then told him to remount his horse and, as we were returning to the command, we found his revolver lying in the grass. I kept his horse and pistol and gave the rifle to a raw recruit and we afterwards paroled him. We killed eight or ten of them and after taking all the provisions that we could carry, we set fire to the wagons and proceeded on our journey south.

About nine o'clock that night, a Federal company came up in our rear and fired on our guard. We immediately formed in line and, after firing a volley or two at them, we then fell back. Then some of our raw recruits became scattered and some of them never did return. We rode all night that night at a lively pace and crossed the Osage River about day-break at the old town of Papinsville. When we had gotten out on the prairie we looked back and saw a regiment of Feedral soildiers following us about five miles in our rear. We rode all day until about 10 o'clock that night, when we stopped and prepared something to eat and fed our horses. We started on the march again next morning at 4 o'clock and went into camp near Lamar in Barton County. There we learned that there was a Captain Lewis with about forty men camped near us and that he was going South the next day. Quantrell sent him word to come over and join us and we would go South together. When Lewis came he suggested that we would go to Lamar that night and capture a Federal company stationed there. Before we got to the town the Federals who had heard we were coming, had gotten into the court-house and we, only having side-arms, could not dislodge them. We had one man, Jim Donohue, killed there. Will Halloran and myself crawled up behind an old frame building and fired into the court-house windows with our revolvers. The Federals poured a volley into the old shop and the flying splinters knocked us both down, one striking me just above the right eye and one striking Halloran in the neck. We were not in Lamar over thirty minutes. During this fight the negro, John Noland, who had been with us since Captain Childs was wounded at Sibley, gave more commands than anyone, calling for general Shelby to come up on the south side and General Marmaduke to come on the west, and ordering the artillery to advance and blow the court-house up, but his talk failed to scare the Federals into surrendering. As we left Lamar, we picked up the body of poor Jim Donohue and, tying it on his horse, we buried him at the mouth of a lane about two miles south of town, building a rail pen around his grave. We then porceeded south into Newton County. There Captain Lewis separated from us, going to the left and we going to the right down into the Indian Territory. We went on into Fort Smith, Arkansas, where we stayed for about ten days, this country then being in the hands of the Confederates. While at Fort Smith, I sold the black mare that I had ridden from Jackson County for $200, Confederate money, keeping the horse that I had captured in Cass County. Leaving Fort Smith, we crossed the Arkansas River at Van Buren, and at Dipper Springs we joined General Marmaduke and General Shelby and our company was attached to Elliott's battalion of cavalry. After remaining in camp about a week the entire command went from there to Cane Hill. While at Cane Hill, Jim Lane and Montgomery, with a large force, got past our pickets and the first intimation we had of their presence was when just at sun-up they fired a cannon right in our camp. Soon learing that they had too much force for us, we retreated across the Boston Mountain. When we had reached the foot of the mountain, Elliott's battallion was put to the right to hold the Federals in check until the baggage train could get up the mountain.

Colonel Quantrell had left us and had turned the command over to Captain Bill Gregg. Quantrell had gone to Richmond, Virginia, and secured his commission as a colonel and command of a batallion of Missourians. I was detailed on the watch. I saw the enemy coming up the creek and, at once, reported to Gregg and Colonel Elliott. Returning to my post, I saw that they were advancing very rapidly and immediately returned to Elliott and Gregg and told them if we stayed there a few minutes longer we would be cut off and would have to cut a hole through the enemy to get out. Colonel Elliott, as soon as he saw our perilous position, ordered a retreat, and, as we crossed the creek, about fifty yards ahead of them, the enemy poured a heavy volley of grape, canister and minie balls at us, and nothing but the poor shooting of the Yankees saved us all from being killed, but only two of Elliott's men were slightly wounded. We kept us a constant firing as we went up the mountains. During this running fight, one of our company, Dick Turpin, became separated from us, and, riding up to where General Shelby was, the general asked him what command he belonged to. He replied "Quantrell's." Shelby replied, "I thought those boys always stayed in their places." To which Turpin replied, "I can go any place you can: come on." The general started to follow, when his horse was killed under him. Turpin turned in his saddle and saw Shelby getting up and said, "General, what in the hell are you stopping there for? Why don't you come on?" Going up the mountain, General Shelby had three horses killed under him. After getting over the mountain, we started down Cole Creek. the baggage train being ahead of us. The Federals closed up and made a saber charge on our rear guard. Captain Gregg then told me to go down the creek and find a place to form, as he wanted to check that charge. I started and took Dave Pool with me and, just past the spur of the mountain, I found a place about large enough for forty men to form on. Leaving Poole there, I rode back and notified Gregg. The boys came on down on the double quick, about half of them forming and the remainder forming in the rear. About that time, Captain John Jarrett, who had formerly been with Quantrell, but who was then in command of a company of cavalry under Shelby, came up and asked me what we were going to do. I told him we were going to check that charge and to get in the rear. Before we had time really to re-form the Federals came to within about thirty yards of us and Captain Gregg gave the command to charge. We rushed forward, yelling and shooting and, at the first volley, we un-horsed thirty-seven of them, among them being a Major Hubbard. The federals immediately turned and went back up the mountain at a more rapid pace than they had come down, we following them about a quarter of a mile, wounding and killing a good many more. When one of the men came up to where Captain Hubbard was lying wounded, he dismounted and took his belt, revolver and sword and a fine, new overcoat that Hubbard was wearing and told him he was going to kill him. Just then General Shelby came along and asked what he was going to do with that man, and being told he was going to kill him, Shelby very sternly, said, "No, you are not. Return

46a

WILLIAM GREGG.

46b

that man his belt, sword, revolver and overcoat," which was very promptly done. In about an hour from this time, the Federals came down with a flag of truce and took up their dead and wounded. We then went into camp near Van Buren and remained in camp about four days, when we learned that General Sterling Price was coming up from the South with his infantry, intending to give battle to the Federals. We then went back to Dripping Springs and waited for General Price. Among the first company to arive were a number of my former friends, whom I had not seen since 1861 and among them my friend Henry Brookins. When we first joined Price at Warrensburg in 1861, Brookins and I had agreed not to have our hair trimmed nor to shave until the war was over. I had kept my promise and when I saw Brookins, he had his hair nicely trimmed and cleanly shaved except a long mustache, and, with my long hair which was then below my shoulders and with my flowing beard, I walked up to him, caught him by the mustache and said, "Henry, you lied to me. Where is that hair?" He said, "They would not let us wear long hair in the South; if we would not have it trimmed they would throw us down and cut it off for us.

The next morning the entire command was ordered north. Tom Harris, Rice and I were detailed to remain and cook up all the provisions we had in our company. We did the cooking, loading the provisions into the wagon, and overtook the company about 2 o'clock in the morning and the boys soon devoured what we had cooked. We then proceeded north, the infantry on the right and the cavalry on the left. Just as the cavalry, Elliott's battallion being in the advance, turned the spur of the mountain, near Prairie Grove, we discovered the advance guard of the enemy getting breakfast. There were a thousand men in this advance guard and just at sunrise, Colonel Elliott ordered us to form in line and charge. We captured about four hundred of them and pursued the remainder to a creek. The weather being very cold the creek banks were frozen and we captured 200 more at the creek and took possession of all their wagons and provisions. We only killed ten or fifteen of them, but wounded several. They never fired a shot at us, being too busy trying to get away. Our battalion was then moved forward and took up a position on a high ridge to the extreme left, from which we could see the infantry of both armies gradually drawing near each other and about 9 o'clock in the morning both sides opened fire and the battle continued all day until dark when we were ordered to fall back. We retreated South to Dripping Springs and stayed there a day or two. Then we were ordered South and so we marhed dowcn into Arkansas. While we were at Van Buren, Arkansas, one of the boys came up to me and said, "John, lets go back to Missouri." "All right," I replied. So six of us started back, including George Wigginton and Ike Bassham. We put on Federal uniforms as the country through which we were to go was full of Federals. On the way back we learned that there was a regiment of Federals at Bowers' Mill, so we decided to pass to the left of Bowers' Mill in order to avoid embarrassing questions that the Federals there might ask us. We had to cross a creek, where we saw several militiamen stationed.

Just before we got to the creek we saw one of the militiamen get on a horse and start in a fast gallop towards Bowers' Mill and we knew that he had gone to report us. We crossed the river and just to the right of the road, we saw a company of militia coming across a little field. They called to me and I answered them when Ike Bassham put spurs to his horse and started to run. I caught his bridle and told him to hold on. The militia did not attempt to follow us so we rode into the woods, and when we reached the edge of the prairie, we saw three different sets of Federal scouts. We stayed in the woods until dark when we rode up to a house. A man came to the door and we asked him if we could get something to eat and feed our horses. He, supposing us to be Federals invited us in and, while we were at the supper table, he told us that he belonged to the militia and that his company was in camp about a mile from the house, and that after supper he was going back and would be glad to have us go with him and spend the night with the boys. We, of course, told him we would be only too glad to do so. After supper, we all started toward the Federal camp, the militiaman and I riding together in front. After getting out a short distance from the house, I suddenly drew my revolver and throwing it to his face, told him to give up his gun, which he handed to one of the other boys. I then said to him, "We are Confederate soldiers; we want you to show us the way to Sim's Point. If you attempt to mislead us, we'll shoot you, and if you take us into a Federal camp, I'll kill you before they can get us. Now show us the way." He said he did not know the way, but I told him he did, and he had to have us at Sims' Point by daylight, or I would shoot him. We rode all night and, just at daylight, we reached Sims' Point and I was well acquainted with a man who lived there. He was in a corn-crib when we rode up and I called to him to come outside. He said, "Well, what in the devil are you doing here?" I said, "It is none of your business what I am doing here; you can come out here, I want to find out something." When he had gotten outside, he saw the militiaman and said, "What in the hell are you doing with that damned Home Guard with you?" I told him to never mind the Home Guard; I was taking care of him, "He'll not bother you any." "But he may bother me after a while." But I told him that this Home Guard would never bother him any more. I then asked him if he knew where there were any Federal soldiers and he said that there were none any nearer than ten miles. We got our breakfast with him and taking feed for our horses with us and also taking the Home Guard along for good company, we went into the woods and stayed until dark and then rode all night long, covering about forty-five miles of road, we reached Calvin's Branch between Pleasant Hill and Harrisonville just about sun-up. Having secured our breakfast, we went down into the woods and stayed until night, where we paroled our prisoner, and going north across Big Creek, we went to the home of my uncle, John Wigginton, arriving there in January, 1863, this being the same place where I had attempted to raise a crop the preceding summer and where on August 11, 1862, I joined Quantrell.

CHAPTER VII.

When we reached the house about 12 o'clock at night, George Wigginton knocked on the door. His mother called, "Who is there?" and when he replied, "George," she sprang out of the bed, opened the door and threw her arms around his neck, kissing him and crying, and to my great delight and surprise, I found my mother there. Oh! How glad these two old mothers were to see their boys whom they did not know were living or dead. My uncle John said to us, "Boys, I am afraid you have done a bad job, coming back here before spring; I doubt very much if you get through the winter. This country is full of Federals. There is a big force at Independence under Colonel Pennock and a regiment at Pleasant Hill and also a regiment at Harrisonville." The next afternoon we went in search of Cole Younger and George Todd and the next day we found them in camp in the woods about seven miles south of Independence on Howard's Branch, and with him were my brother, Jabez, Tom Tally, George Tally, Joe Hardin, Doc Hale and Jim Morris and in a few days Ike Bassham and three others joined us. We then dug a pit or cave in the side of the hill and covered it with logs, old boards and brush, with a fireplace in the back with a chimney made of sticks and mud. This was a warm place to stay, but we cooked only at night for fear the Federals would locate us by the smoke from our camp. Cole Younger and his men had a similar den about twenty feet from ours. One night while we were here, George Wigginton and I decided we would ride over and see our mothers, who were both at his father's. As we came to the edge of the prairie, noticing several fires, we stopped our horses and counted seventeen houses belonging to Southern men burning, and among them was the house of Wigginton's father. Imagine our feelings—both of our old mothers were then being thrown out of shelter in the dead of winter. We sat on our horses and watched them burn. Wigginton, who was always a very quiet man, sat with his eyes fixed on his father's home and I said to him, "George, what do you think now?" He turned to me and said, "Well John, I think, 'Damn it.'" After we had been in camp about ten days, John McDowell came into our camp. He had gone south with us, being a member of Captain Jarrett's company and, as soon as he returned to Jackson County, had gone direct to Independence and surrendered to Colonel Pennock and been paroled. As soon as he came into camp, I suspicioned him, for the reason that Pennock had never been known to parole a Southern man before. I told Cole Younger he was a traitor and we ought to get rid of him but Younger would not believe it. In a few days Captain George Todd came into our camp and I spoke to him about McDowell and he agreed with me, but Younger would not consent to our doing anything to him. A heavy snow had fallen and a crust had formed, making the traveling exceedingly bad. McDowell told Younger that he wanted to go over to John Garrison's to see his wife who was there. I objected and said to Younger, in the presence of McoDwell, "Cole, do not let him go. He is a traitor and will get us into trouble, and if I was in command of this squad, he would not be John McDowell much longer, for I would either hang him or shoot him. You know and John McDowell knows that old Pennock never released a rebel soldier before and has made arrangements with him to betray us, so either shoot or hang the traitor." Younger replied, "John, you are too hard on him; he's all right. He went South with Jarrett." I told him that might be true but that I knew he was a traitor and a spy and was a liar about his wife and just as soon as he gets out of our sight, he will run his horse to Independence and tell Pennock where we are. But Cole let him go. After McDowell had been gone a while, we were trying to catch some hogs that were running in the woods and had left our pistols inn our den, when one of the boys yelled out, "The Federals are coming." I looked up and saw about sixty men coming afoot and only about fifty yards from us. Some of the boys said, "They are not Federals, but George Todd's men." I said, "What the devil is George Todd doing coming afoot; break for your weapons boys." The Federals then called to us, "Don't be alarmed, we are friends." Then Cole Younger fired at them and they fired on us. I sprang into the den, jerked my revolver from a rafter and told the boys to get out. As I rushed out of the den, I attempted to fire on them, but my pistol snapped. We all scattered. Ike aBssham was killed just as he came out of the door. Joe Hardin fell dead within about ten feet of the door and Doc Hale and George Tally were killed about a hundred yards from the camp. I started on a run through the brush, the Federals firing at me all of the time. I ran over a log and fell down, but got up running, the bullets making snow fly all around me. I crossed a little branch and someone called to me and said "John, wait." I turned and it was George Wigginton. Just back of George was a negro militiaman, running after him; George wheeled and killed the negro, and said "John, let's turn and fight them." I told him that we had better save our loads until the last and get away if we could. Just then another man called me and, as he had on a Federal cap, I started to shoot him, when he called again and I recognized Jim Morris. He also wanted to stop and fight them. I asked him where his pistols were and he said he had lost them. I then advised him that the best thing that he could do was to get in front of us and do some of his best running. We came to a little clearing and, as we started across, several Federals fired at us, and I noticed blood on the snow, and Morris looked at his hand, around which we tied a handkerchief to keep the blood from leaving a trail in the snow. We kept on until we came to the creek, where there were a good many cattle paths. We got into one of these paths and followed it for a while and then we went into the brush and on through the woods to Carroll Johnson's house, and there we secured two horses from

Johnson, promising him to return them as soon as we could find some of our own, and George Wigginton and Morris rode one horse and we started to find Captain Todd's camp. When we reached the house of John Prewitt, we were nearly frozen, and so hoarse we could hardly speak above a whisper. We stopped at his house a short while and then went on in search of George Todd's camp.

When the Federals fired on us at our den, my brother Jabez received a scalp wound and, while it was not very serious, it bled very freely. He and Cole Younger ran together, and he had on a pair of heavy cavalry boots. From the loss of blood and trying to run with heavy boots on, he became very tired and told Cole that he could not stand it much longer. He sat down on the snow and while ten or fifteen Federals were shooting at them, Cole pulled my brother's boots off. He then jumped up and ran through the snow and ice in his stocking feet. In this little skirmish, they killed four of our boys and we killed seven white men and one negro for them. We afterwards learned that this man, John McBride, had made an agreement with Colonel Pennock that he was to receive $1,000 for Cole Younger, $500 each for myself and my brother and $100 each for either of the other boys, the money to be paid for our delivery to him or his men, either dead or alive, and they well knew that there was very little chance of any of us being delivered alive.

After leaving Mr. Prewitt's, Wigginton, Morris and I went across the Blue, where we found Craid Wells and John Blythes in a dugout on the side of a bank. We stayed there ten days. Wells' sisters and mother came at night to where we were and brought us food from the house. After the snow had melted, Wigginton and I started back to learn how many of the boys had been killed and wounded. On this trip I received word from Travis Morgan that he had a fine four year old saddle stallion in a barn about a mile from Independence, and a good saddle and bridle in the loft, and I was willing to run the risk of being captured, I could have him. Accompanied by Will Hulse, I secured the horse, saddle and bridle and came back to his father's house, secured a late supper and Will's sister, Miss Sallie, presented me with a quart bottle of blackberry cordial. In a few days George Wigginton captured him a horse and we returned Johnson's horses to him. At this time, George Todd had ten men under his command and Cole Younger sixteen in his command. We continued to sleep in the woods at night and eat with our friends, and William Hopkins invited us all to meet at his house on February 14, 1863, and to enjoy a big turkey dinner. On the morning of the thirteenth of February, Captain Wagner came out of Independence with sixty-four men from the Fifth Missouri State Militia, looking for us, and went into camp in Mr. Hines' yard, whose son Jim was with us. That night twelve of us went to Hines' with the intention of firing on the militia, but before reaching there I suggested to Cole Younger that if we did, they would probably kill Mr. Hines and burn his house. We abandoned the trip and went back into the woods. On that morning, Captain John Jarrett and

John Roth had returned from the South and joined us. When the morning of the 14th of February came Cole Younger suggested that if we expected to enjoy our turkey dinner we had better first get rid of Captain Wagner and his militia. The house of William Hopkins was on a high bluff and his father, Dick Hopkins, lived on the opposite side of the bottom on a high bluff. We agreed that Cole Younger should go with his men on the bluff near Will Hopkins' house at a point where the roads made a sharp turn around the bluff and John Barrett and John Roth should ride out where the militia could see them and when the militia attempted to capture them, make a rush to this place of ambush. When we reached the point near Will Hopkins' house, we met Captain Todd and his ten men and he took command and ordered us to form a line back from the road on the top of the hill. In a short time, we saw Barrett and Roth coming at full speed with the militia in full pursuit. When they had gotten into the cut, Barrett and Roth rushed around the turn and joined us. Captain Wagner ordered his company in the cut between the bluff and the high rail fence and he and his first lieutenant rode around in sight of us. Captain Todd, who was standing in front of our lines, fired at him. Wagner raised his hand with his revolver in it and shouted, "Don't fire, men, we are Federal soldiers and belong to the artillery; don't you see the brass on my saddle?" Todd replied, "To hell with your artillery; kill them boys, kill them." I was standing near Captain Todd at the time with a double barrelled shot-gun, with each barrel loaded with fifteen pistol balls. I fired at Captain Wagner. Several of the balls struck his horse and one cut his little finger off, causing him to drop his revolver. Todd then yelled "Charge." They became bunched up between the fence and the bluff and we were right on them before they could get their horses to running, and emptying saddles at every jump the horses made, they soon left the road and ran into the woods and into a V-shaped place, where a drainage ditch entered the Little Blue. Some of them forced their horses into the Little Blue and into the ditch. The water in the Blue was very deep and their horses were soon swimming. I rode up to the bank of the Blue and, emptying the other barrel of my shotgun at them, dropped the gun and emptied my revolvers. In this company of militia, there was a man by the name of Jim Lane, who before leaving Independence had said, "Before I return I will either kill a damned bushwhacker or one of their Southern sympathizers." When he reached the Blue, he turned and forced his horse into the ditch and was trying to force him up the opposite bank. Boone Shull saw him and yelled, "Boys, there goes the fellow that was going to kill 'a damned bushwhacker,'" and fired. Lane fell dead and Shull jumped off his own horse remarking, "That's too fine a horse to let get away," and ran into the ditch and captured the horse. Captain Todd then gave command to reload quick and tried to head them at Blue Springs.

While we were reloading an old hypocrite, who under the guise of a Northern Methodist minister had been going over that country, robbing Southern people with the Redlegs and militia, rode up on a mule. He would go to the home of Southern people and hold family prayers with them and then charge them for divine service and, if they had no money, he would by force take their bedding, silverware or anything else of value, and at the time, he had a roll of blankets and comforts and two silk dresses and some silverware that he had forced Mrs. Stanley, the wife of Judge Stanley, to give him that morning. A short time before this, this old hypocrite, with a gang of militia, had gone to the house of Judge Stanley and demanded money from him. Upon the failure of the Judge to comply with their demands, they had burned his feet, pulled his fingernails out and struck him over the head with their revolvers until he had lost his mind, and when this sanctimonious old hypocrite came riding up to us, Jim Little, who knew him too well, rode up to him and asked him what he wanted. The preacher, thinking we were Federal soldiers, told Jim that he had been up and stayed all night at Judge Stanley's, and, hearing the firing, had ridden down to see about it. Jim said to him, "You are the old devil we have been looking for. You have been going around this country praying with Southern people and in every one of your pretended prayers you would offer an insult to the South, and demanding pay, and when you were refused, you would rob defenceless women and children by taking what little property they had and you now have blankets and dresses belonging to Judge Stanley's wife, and now we've got you." The preacher said, "I have a right to have pay for my divine services and ought to be paid for praying for sinners." Jim remarked, "Well, you'd better be praying for yourself, and get at it damned quick." The preacher asked him if he would kill a minister of the gospel. Jim said, "No, but I am going to kill a damned thief and old hypocrite," and shot him and his mule. We afterwards came back and got what he had and took them back and delivered them to Mrs. Stanley.

We then wheeled our horses and tried to intercept the remaining militia at Blue Springs. When we reached the road leading into Blue Springs, they had just passed and would have succeeded in slipping up on them if it had not been for Jim Little, who began to yell. The militia looked back and began to whip their horses with their rifles and, in a few minutes, we were close enough to open fire on them, following them through the town of Blue Springs. About three quarters of a mile from the town of Blue Springs, there was a very bad mud hole in the road and there had been a number of poles laid across it, and, when the militia reached this place, their horses going in a run, quite a number of their horses stumbled and fell, piling men and horses in one promiscuous heap and ten of the militia ceased to bother us from that time on. We continued to follow them until they had reached the bridge across the Little Blue when Captain Wagner rode on to the bridge ahead of them and, drawing his revolver, commanded them to halt and face us, saying that he would shoot the first man who attempted to ride by him, to which command one of his men replied, "There's a damned sight more danger behind us than in front of us." We fired at them again and wheeled our horses, riding back. We afterwards learned that out of the sixty-four men that had left Independence with Captain Wagner, only seven ever returned, and two of that number were badly wounded. Just before we reached the mud hole, one of the militiamen fell off his horse in a fence corner. Mart Belt, who had been following him and shooting at him, rode up to him took his pistols away from him and, leading the militiaman's horse, came galloping up to the rest of us and said, "Boys, I got that fellow all right." Some of the boys, who knew that Mart was a poor pistol shot, laughed at him and told him he couldn't hit a barn. Mart said, "Wait until we go back, and I'll show you where I shot him in the side of the head." When we got back to the place where the man had fallen, there was no man there, and an old gentleman, who lived nearby, came out into his yard and Mart asked him what had become of that dead man. The old man replied, "Dead man, Hell! If you'd have seen him running through that field after you boys rode off, you wouldn't have taken him for a corpse." We rode back to Will Hopkins' and arrived there at two o'clock in the afternoon, and did ample justice to a fine turkey dinner.

This had been a good day's work; twenty-seven of us had routed a company of sixty-four, killed fifty-seven of them and none of our men were wounded, and at this time, there were seven thousand Federal soldiers in Jackson county and a large

Federal force in Lexington, Harrisonville and Pleasant Hill, and our little bunch of twenty-seven men, who were the only armed Confederates in that part of the country, caused all these soldiers to stay there and kept them from following General Price.

After dinner at Will Hopkins', we separated again and remained in hiding for about ten days, when Cole Younger, John Jarrett, Captain Scott, Jim Noland and I went down into Lafayette county and stopped at the house of my uncle, William Fristoe. The next morning we started out on the road to intercept the stage, running from Lexington to Warrensburg. We had a two-fold object in wanting to intercept this stage; one was that the Federal officers made frequent trips in this stage and we were anxisou to see them, and, if possible, to secure a newspaper, and, when the stage come in sight, we halted it and we found Colonel King, son of Ex-Governor King and another Federal officer, who was a provost-marshal from Lexington. We afterwards learned that when we first halted them, the provost-marshal took the star from his hat on which there was a number "5", for he well knew that No. 5 meant death, because that was the number of old Pennock's regiment. When we had made them get out of the stage, Colonel King asked what we intended to with them, and Captain Scott told him, "Kill you, of course," to which King remarked, "That is a strange way to carry on civil war." Captain Scott walked up to him and, putting his hand on his shoulder, said, "Colonel, that is the fault of your side; whenever you fight us, you always carry a black flag; our Colonel, Quantrell, has made overtures to you to exchange prisoners and has always been refused, and you troops are instructed to take none of us prisoners, but to either hang or shoot us as soon as captured, and, in addition to that, you murder all of the old men, who sympathize with the South and burn and destroy all their property, and we are only retaliating." About that time, John Jarrett walked up and, Colonel King, seeing a Masonic pin on Jarrett, let him know he was a Mason. Jarrett then said, "Hold on, boys," and, turning to Colonel King, said "What Captain Scott has told you is true; we only kill the men who kill us and our friends; we do not burn houses and we do not rob Union citizens, for if we did, our Colonel would have us shot. Now, if you will promise me to do all in your power to have this burning stopped, we will release you." Colonel King made him the promise and they were released, and I must say to his credit that, for two or three months, the burning ceased. We stayed with our friends until April, when Colonel Quantrell returned from the South with the remainder of our company.

On his way back from the South, Colonel Quantrell came by way of Spring River to have a little interview with that hartless old murderer, Colonel Obediah Smith, who had done so much murdering and burning in that part of the state. When Quantrell rode up to Smith's house, he found him in the garden, having a rifle with him and, as Quantrell and his men were all wearing blue overcoats, Smith came to the fence. Quantrell shook hands with him and told him that that was a very fine rifle he had and that he would like to see it. Smith handed him the rifle, remarking, "Yes, and I've turned many a damed rebel over with it." Quantrell pointed the gun at him and pulled the trigger, but the gun snapped. Smith took the hint, ran around his house and jumped into a stable lot, and when he was about to reach the fence on the opposite side of the lot, Bill McGuire shot at him and Obadiah Smith never turned over another rebel. Colonel Quantrell told me that in his trip from the South, he had no trouble passing the Federal pickets, as he passed himself off as Colonel Clark, of a Colorado regiment. We waited around in hiding, waiting for the leaves to get thick on the trees and in the brush. One day Cole Younger rode over to see his Grandmother Fristoe and hitched his mare in the orchard. While he was talking to his grandmother, a negro woman came and told him the Federals were ocming. Cole beat a hasty retreat but had to leave his mare, which the Federals captured. Quantrell then ordered my brother, Jabez McCorkle, and me to hunt the boys up and get them together. I had a squad with me under a bluff on Cedar Creek, and one morning before I dressed Jabez came up with a squad and, leaving his men, came to where I was and was standing on a rock, when in some way he dropped a Springfield rifle which he had in his hand, discharging it, the ball striking him in the right leg just below the knee and, passing upward, shattered the knee joint. We placed him on a blanket and carried him under a bluff and waited on him for several days, but fearing the Federals might discover him, we moved him over on the Nelson Creek and

FRANK JAMES.

64b

made him a bed under a bluff. His wife and sister stayed with him where he lingered thirteen days and died, and, when the end came, his mother-in-law, Mrs. Harris, his wife, and sister and I were with him. In this sad manner ended the life of my only brother, a brave, true man and soldier. It seems strange that, having passed through so many dangerous places, he had to die at last from a wound inflicted by his own gun. Just after he died, Frank James, Captain Scott and Tom Harris came to where we were. This was the first time I had ever seen Frank James, and when he rode up to where my dead brother was lying, he remarked, "We heard he was here wounded and had come to stay with him to keep the Federals from finding and killing him." That night, we took his body to his mother-in-law's house, leaving only the women to watch with him and the men all returned to the woods, waiting for the coffin to be made. While his corpse was lying in Harris' house, a company of Federal troops came in, looked at the corpse and left. The next day, he was buried in a country grave-yard near the house, where a few years before, he had been married. Soon after the death of brother, one of our bravest men, Jim Vaughan, was in Wyandotte, Kansas, and, while being shaved in a barber shop, the Federals rushed in on him and captured him, taking him into Kansas City, where they placed him in prison. General Buell, after learning who he was, ordered him to be hung within ten days. In a few days after his capture, we captured three Union soldiers, a lieutenant, an orderly sergeant and a private. Quantrell told a Union citizen to go to Kansas

City and to see Colonel Buell and to tell him that if he would exchange Vaughan for the three Federals we had, that he would send the three Union soldiers to Kansas City unharmed, but if he carried out his intention to hang Vaughan, then the three Federals would be either hung or shot. The next day, this citizen returned to Kansas City and, in the presence of our three prisoners, reported that the Federal commander had refused to exchange Vaughan and was going to hang him. The lieutenant left the other prisoners and, walking up to Quantrell, said, "Colonel, I know you intend to execute me and my two companions and, after knowing you have tried to save us, I do not blame you, but I have a proposition to make to you: if you will let me, I will go to Kansas City and see the authorities and, I believe, that being a lieutenant in the regular army, I may be able to prevail upon them to accept your proposition, and I now promise you, upon my honor, that I will return, whatever may be their decision." Quantrell looked at him a moment and said, "I will trust you; go." On the afternoon of the third day, the lieutenant rode into our camp and, walking straight up to our colonel, said, "I have failed; I gave you my word, and I have returned to be executed, and am prepared to die. I do not blame you, Colonel, and I do not believe that if you had fifty of our best men, they would exchange Vaughan for all of them, so, Colonel, we await your orders." Quantrell looked at him a moment, making no reply, turning on his heel, called Cole Younger, Frank James and myself to him, and taking us to one side, said, "Boys, this man is too honorable and brave to die; he has done all in his power to save Jim Vaughan, and I believe that either one of the others would have done the same thing, and they ought not to suffer for the brutality and meanness of others, and I'll be damed if any of them shall die by my hand." He then sent for the three prisoners and said to them, "Boys, your lieutenant is too honorable and brave a man to die and I believe you are all that way. There is not one man in ten thousand who would have acted as your lieutenant has. Now, if you'll give me your word of honor, and I know your lieutenant is a man of honor, that you will never again take up arms against the South, I am going to let you go. My men and I may be outlaws, but we are honorable and have some heart left and have never yet murdered a brave man." The three Federal soldiers, with tears in their eyes, thanked Colonel Quantrell, mounted their horses and left, and we afterwards learned that they went into Kansas City, reported these facts to the commander and resigned from the service, going back home, but nevertheless, the next morning, Jim Vaughan was hung. As they led him out to the scaffold, with his head erect, he said, "You may kill me, but you'll never conquer me, and taking my life today will cost you a hundred lives and this debt my friends will pay in a short time." And how prophetic his last words were will soon be seen.

A short time after the execution of Vaughan, Quantrell took about half of his company and went down on the Sni, leaving the remainder of us under the command of Captain George Todd, and, on the seventeenth day of June, 1863, we discovered a company of Federals crossing the prairie in the direction of Westport. We turned into the woods and, following Brush Creek, entered the town of Westport on the south. On the southeast side of this town there was a lane, which had a high rock fence on either side. When we reached this lane, we formed in platoons of eight and waited for them. They came riding very leisurely over the hill, the captain in front, with his leg thrown over his horse's neck. He asked who we were when Captain Todd yelled, "Charge, kill 'em, boys, kill 'em," which we immediately proceeded to do. We charged them in the lane, yelling and shooting as we rode. They were thrown into a perfect stampede and rushed out on to the open prairie. While we were running them, I saw two of them leave their horses and I tried to get some rocks off the fence so my horse could get over. Bill McGuire rode up to me and said, "My horse will take the fence," so putting spurs to his horse, he went over the fence and followed them, returning with their guns and pistols. Boone Sholl, who was riding the horse that he had taken from Jim Lane near Blue Springs, lost control of his horse, which ran away with him and through the line of Federals, who shot him in the back, the ball passing through his body and breaking the buckle on his belt. We found that we had killed thirty-three of them. Will McGuire rode up to a dead Federal officer who had assisted in the hanging of Jim Vaughan, and wrote upon a slip of paper, "Remember the dying words of Jim

Vaughan," and placed it in the teeth of the dead Federal.

Sholl held up and rode his horse about nine miles that night, and was taken to the home of a widow by the name of Young, where he died the next morning, and, just before he died, he told the boys that he wanted Captain Todd to have his horse. During this fight in the lane, Al Wyatt's horse also became unmanageable and ran into the Federals. Wyatt was shot in the breast and instantly killed. He had only been with us a few days. I took his spurs and sent them to his wife. After the Federals had left the lane and we had quit following them, they began to fire at us and one of the balls struck Captain Scott in the neck. He threw up his hands, exclaming, "I am a dead man," and fell from his horse. These three men, Captain Scott, Al Wyatt and Boone Sholl, were the only men we lost. Not another one of our men was even wounded. We tied the bodies of Captain Scott and Al Wyatt across their saddles and, leading their horses, took them to a graveyard, and, wrapping their blankets around them, buried them.

CHAPTER IX.

We then went into camp on Cedar Creek at a rendezvous we called the "bull-pen." This was situated in the dense woods about a mile from Cedar Creek. There were two ways of approaching the "bull pen," one through the bottom and the other through the woods south of John Moore's farm. We never approached this camp together, nor left it together, always going separately in different directions, in this way leaving no trail and this camp never was discovered by the Federals until after the war.

We stayed in this camp for four or five days waiting to hear from Colonel Quantrell. In a few days, we went with Captain Todd down on the Sni and joined Quantrell. Dave Poole took forty of us with him and went down in what was known as the Dutch settlement in Lafayette County, near Concordia. There was stationed there a company of Dutch militia, who had a fort or blockhouse near the town, and, whenever any strangers were seen in that neighborhood, they would blow the dinner horns and ring the bells all running for the blockhouse, and when we reached there, we found them all securely fortified in the blockhouse, and having only side arms with us, we left them alone, and securing a number of extra good horses, we returned to the Sni. In a few days, we went over to Olathe, Kansas, and captured a Federal major and found a Mexican wagon-train. We did not molest the Mexicans, but I traded hats with the wagon master and also traded my Colt's revolver for a dragoon pistol.

One morning Captain Todd, with about twenty of us, started south to Big Creek, and, at a point where the town of Lee's Summit is now located, we met a company of thirty Federals and before they had time to form in line, we charged them and they scattered and we chased them on the prairie, killing seven of them. Captain Todd was riding a horse that Boone Sholl had left him and the horse acted the same way that he did with Sholl, running off with him and right through the Federals, Todd receiving a slight wound in his arm. Todd then wanted to trade horses with me, but I told him that I didn't want anything to do with that damned Yankee horse, that he had as well kill him as me, but, after the captain had offered me sufficient inducements, I finally traded with him. We went back to Pleasant Hill and from there to Chapel Hill in Johnson County. There were six or eight of us riding in advance, when we encountered twelve or fifteen Federals and charged them. They formed in line and fired, killing Bill Greenwood's horse, which fell, throwing Bill over its head. Before Bill had time to regain his feet a Federal soldier rode up to him and, drawing his revolver, commanded Bill to hand over his pistols. Greenwood, who had the reputation of being one of the best and quickest pistol shots in the company, replied, "All right," and drawing his pistols, fired. The Federal fell; Bill grabbed his horse by the bridle and swinging himself into the saddle, came galloping up, remarking, "Boys, I made a good horse trade." We went back on the Sni and rejoined Quantrell. We went from there to Bone Hill and from there to Sibley, on the Missouri River. While at Sibley, we saw a militiaman standing in the door of a house across the Missouri river. I drew my big dragoon pistol, that I had gotten from the Mexican, I fired at the militiaman, who very promptly left the door and I afterwards learned from a friend that the ball buried itself just over his head in the door.

We then returned to the Little Blue and separated. One morning, Will Bassham asked me to go over to his uncle's, Jack Bassham's with him. While we were waiting for our breakfast to be cooked, Will went into another room to change his clothes and I was to stand in the door and watch for Federals. Mr. Bassham had two daughters, Miss Annie and Miss Maisie. Miss Annie came to the door and was talking with me, and, being very pretty and very attractive, my attention was on her and not on the Federals. After we had stood there a few moments, her mother called her and, as soon as she had left the door, to my utter surprise, nine Federals rose from behind a clump of bushes, not over forty yards from me and fired at me. This was the first intimation I had of their presence. I called to Bill to get out quick. We sprang on our horses and dashed across the field and the Federals yelled at us, "Oh, damn you, we'll eat your breakfast for you." When we came on the road leading to Blue Springs, we met Captain Todd, Lee McMurty and Will Hulse. Hulse and I then rode in front and he exclaimed, stopping his horse, "Yonder is a damned Yankee kneeling in the brush," and we both fired at him and then turned and went back. At this time the Federals, in groups of fifteen or twenty were scouring that country watching for us, guarding all the fords and crossroads and the houses of all our friends, which kept us constantly on the lookout. After shooting at the Yankee, we went to the house of a friend, Jim Woods, to see if we could not have better luck getting our breakfast, but, just as we got to Woods' yard, we found another squad of Federals there ahead of us. We exchanged a few shots with them and left and about 11 o'-

clock, succeeded in getting something to eat at the Widow Dillingham's. About this time, Cole Younger decided that he just must see his sweetheart, a Miss Lizzie Brown who lived about two miles northwest of Harrisonville, and so he persuaded Tom Tally, Will Hulse, George Wigginton and George Jackson and myself to go with him and act as his bodyguard and to protect him while he talked to his sweetheart. We stayed in this neighborhood for about a week, Cole going to see his girl every day and every night. We had no trouble on this trip, although we were within two miles of three hundred Federals who were located in Harrisonville. Going back to Big Creek, we started across the prairie to Hickory Grove, and when we had reached a high point on the road leading from Kansas City to Lone Jack, we saw a regiment of Federal soldiers, which we afterwards learned was the Seventh Kansas Cavalry. As soon as they saw us, they started in pursuit and followed us six miles across the prairie. When we had reached the top of another ridge, Cole Younger said, "Hold up, boys, they have run a mile, while we've only run a half. Hold your horses back and save them for the dash in the woods." He and I dropped back behind the boys, trying to hold them in check and when we had gotten within half a mile of the timber, Cole yelled, "Now give your horses their heads." We soon were in the brush, when Cole wheeled his horse and waved his hat and told them now to come on, but they refused to follow us into the woods. The next day Colonel Quantrell himself took command and we went over to Pink Hill, and being informed that on Texas Prairie, which was about ten miles distant, there was a company of Federals, we went in that direction, but when we got there, we found that it was a regiment instead of a company, and as soon as they saw us, they started after us and followed us ten or twelve miles across the Sni and on to Little Blue. When about a mile from the Little Blue, having gotten over the brow of a hill, Quantrell ordered us to form in line, about face and charge them. This checked them and they turned and went back towards Lexington. We killed several of them. We scattered that evening in order to get our supper and while one of our men, Jim Tucker, was eating his supper, they captured him. They took him to where the company was camped and kept him all night and the next morning about daylight, Tucker and his guard were a little distance from the company, when Tucker suddenly wheeled on him, struck him with his fist, knocked him down and dashing into the brush, escaped. They fired a number of shots at him, but he was not struck, and when he returned to camp, he composed a song, using the tune of that old negro song, "Run, nigger, run, or the pat-er-ole'll catch you," and the chorus of his song was:

Run, Jim run, or the Feds will cetch you,
They shot ten times and never tetched you.

We went from there over to the Missouri river at a point between Wellington and Sibley and, during the night, we saw a steamboat coming up the Missouri river. We hitched our horses in the brush, and concealed ourselves on the bank near a bend in the river. When the boat was opposite us, Quantrell hailed the boat and ordered the captain to land or we would sink the boat, and when she landed, we ordered the stage plank lowered and went aboard. We found aboard about a dozen Kansas soldiers and a good many negroes. The Kansas soldiers and the negroes were paroled and, after taking a number of horses, and throwing the Government supplies overboard, we then let the boat and the passengers proceed on their way. This boat was called the Sam Gatey. John Ross captured a very fine sorrel stallion that was being shipped to a Federal officer at Kansas City and gave him the name of the boat.

In September, 1863, Captain Bill Anderson and his company joined us. At this time, the outrages committed by the Federal troops, which consisted mostly of Home Guards and Kansas Redlegs and Jayhawkers, beggars description. At this late day, it seems impossible that human beings could have been guilty of such merciless outrages as these men mitted. Among the leaders of these bands were Jennison, Jim Lane and a Captain Mead and I will only attempt to give a few of their acts as an illustration of their brutality and to further impress upon the minds of my readers why we acted as we did. Captain Mead, with his band went to the home of Mrs. Carter, a widow seventy years of age, and compelled her, at the hour of 12 o'clock at night to ride fourteen miles horseback, facing a bitter snowstorm, to the town of Independence, where she was lodged in jail for feeding rebel soldiers, her two boys being in the Confederate Army.

About this time, the Federal soldiers at Kansas City, under the command of General Ewing, were guilty of one of the most brutal and fiendish acts that ever disgraced a so-called civilized nation. My sister, Mrs. Charity Kerr and my sister-in-law, Mrs. Nannie McCorkle, the widow of my brother, Jabez, went to Kansas City in a wagon, driving a yoke of oxen, with a load of wheat to exchange it for flour, the women then having all the buying to do. When they had procured their flour and were ready to start home, Anderson Cowgill, a neighbor, who had known these girls all their lives, and the same man who refused to speak to me when we paroled him at Independence, saw these two girls and reported to the authorities that these two women were rebels and were buying flour to feed the bushwhackers. They were immediately arrested and placed in jail with some other girls, who had been arrested and sentenced to be banished and here I copy the following description of what occurred as given by Mrs. Flora Stevens, as she stood at the grave of Josephine Anderson and published in the Kansas City Post, under date of May 2, 1912:

"There were nine of these girls in the prison at 1409 Grand Avenue, when it fell. One of these was Josephine Anderson. Her two sisters, Mollie, aged sixteen, and Janie, ten years old, were also prisoners with her, and it was these three especially that the Union soldiers wanted to kill because they were sisters of Bill Anderson, the guerrila. The others were Mrs. Susan Vandiver, Mrs. Armenia Whitsett-Gilvey and Mrs. Christie McCorkle Kerr, all of whom

Three Years With Quantrell

were killed and Miss Mollie Cranstaff, now Mrs. William Clay, Miss Sue Mundy, now Mrs. N. M. Womacks of Blue Springs and Mrs. Nan Harris McCorkle. The last three escaped with serious injuries. These girls, none of whom were more than twenty years old, had been arrested and brought in by the Union soldiers because they were Southern sympathizers and were being held in prison while waiting to be banished. When the soldiers heard that Bill Anderson's sisters were in their power, they determined to kill them. The first inkling of the plot was when Mrs. B. F. Duke, who now lives at 1717 Wabash avenue, but who then had a boarding house at Independence Avenue and Oak Street, heard some of the soldiers who were staying at her house speak of the progress they were making in tearing down a wall. Mrs. Duke was a cousin of Bill Anderson, but the soldiers did not know it and told her of their scheme, and how they had removed a large section of the foundation wall of the woman's prison. General Bingham, the owner of the building, had protested, they said, but it did not stop them. The building did not fall the first day, so more of the wall was removed and it was at this time that Mrs. Duke learned of it. She was beside herself with rage and ordered all the soldiers from the house. With a number of friends she hurried to the military headquarters and begged that the girls be taken from the building before they were killed. Their pleadings were in vain and an hour later the building fell. The girls had been uneasy by hearing the people on the floor below moving out their stock of groceries and whisky which they took to a safe place. The plastering had been falling all day and the girls were in a panic. Nan Harris and Mollie Anderson had just gone out into the hall for a bucket of water, when they heard cries from the other girls that the roof was falling. The guard, evidently repenting at the last moment, carried these two girls to safety. Janie Anderson, who was the youngest, tried to escape through a window, but a twelve pound ball that had been chained to her ankle held her back and both her legs were broken. The other girls went down with the ruins. There were groans and screams for a long time, and Josephine Anderson could be heard calling for someone to take the bricks off her head. Finally her cries ceased."

This foul murder was the direct cause of the famous raid on Lawrence, Kansas. We could stand no more. Imagine, if you can, my feelings. A loved sister foully murdered and the widow of a dead brother seriously hurt by a set of men to whom the name assassins, murderers and cutthroats would be a compliment. People abuse us, but, my God, did we not have enough to make us desperate and thirst for revenge? We tried to fight like soldiers, but were declared outlaws, huntd under a black flag and murdered like beasts. The homes of our friends burned, our aged sires, who dared sympathize with us had been either hung or shot in the presence of their famalies and all their furniture and provisions loaded in wagons and with our live stock taken to the state of Kansas. The beautiful farming country of Jackson county, Cass County and Johnson County were worse than desert.

and on every hillside stood lone blackened chimneys, sad sentinels and monuments to the memory of our once happy homes. And these outrages had been done by Kansas troops, calling themselves soldiers, but a disgrace to the name soldier. And now our innocent and beautiful girls had been murdered in a most foul, brutal, savage and damnable manner. We were determined to have revenge, and so, Colonel Quantrell and Captain Anderson planned a raid on Lawrence, Kansas, the home of the leaders, Jim Lane and Jennison.

CHAPTER X.

We were all in camp in our headquarters on the banks of the Sni. Colonel Quantrell and Captain Anderson were getting the boys together for the raid on Lawrence, Kansas. The day before they started to Lawrence, Colonel Quantrell sent Andy Blount with fifteen men down into Johnson County in order to attract the Federal forces in that direction. After the fifteen men left with Blount, there still remained with Colonel Quantrell and Anderson about 150 men. On the morning of the 20th of August, Quantrell gave the order to break camp and march in a southwesterly direction, and went over on the Big Blue to a point south of Little Santa Fe, a town just on the Kansas line. His entire march until he reached the Kansas line was through smoking ruins and blackened fields. He halted in the woods all day and just about dark he gave the order to mount and crossed into Kansas at a point about ten miles south of Little Santa Fe and turned directly west toward the town of Lawrence, and, riding all night, the town was reached just at daylight. At the entrance to the town, there were a lot of tents in which were camped a detachment of negro soldiers and a few white men. The command halted here and someone fired a shot. Immediately the negroes and white men rushed out of their tents, the majority of them starting in the direction of the river and some going in the direction of town. The command was given to break ranks, scatter and follow them. A few of the negroes reached the river, plunging into it, but none succeeded in reaching the opposite shore. The troops then dashed back up into the town, down the main street, shooting at every blue coat that came in sight. Just before entering the town Colonel Quantrell turned to his men and said, "Boys, this is the home of Jim Lane and Jennison; remember that in hunting us they gave no quarter. Shoot every soldier you see, but in no way harm a woman or a child." He dashed ahead of his command down Main Street, firing his pistol twice, dismounted from his horse and went into the hotel, where he was met by the landlord, whom he recognized as an old friend and immediately gave orders for the landlord not to be molested and stayed in the hotel and guarded him. During all this time, his command were busy hunting men with blue clothes and setting fire to the town. Jim Lane and Jennison were the ones wanted and some of the boys dashed at once to Jim Lane's house, but, unfortunately for the world, did not find him. They found his saber, which was very handsome, the scab-

TOM LITTLE.

80b

bard being heavily gold-plated. In the parlor of Lane's house, there were three pianos and the boys recognized two of them as having belonged to Southern people in Jackson County, and a great many other things belonging to Southern people were found in his house. Quantrell remained in Lawrence about two hours and when he left, the town was in ashes and 175 Jayhawkers were dead. Lane and Jennison had made desolate the border counties of Missouri, pillaged and burned homes, murdered Southern men, insulted, outraged and murdered the wives and sisters of these men. Quantrell and his command had come to Lawrence to be avenged and they were. In this raid, a few innocent men may have been killed but this was not intentional.

As the command left the town, they discovered a command of Federals coming in pursuit. The whole face of the earth looked blue. One of Quantrell's men returned to the town and was literally riddled with bullets. The command then turned south, with the Federals still in close pursuit and having gone about two miles, stopped at a big house. There was no one at home, but the doors were open and one of the rooms was fitted up as a doctor's office, a lot of bottles and medicine setting on the shelves. The boys knocked the medicine all down and soon the house was afire, a case of spontaneous combustion. Tom Hamilton and another one of boys were wounded in Lawrence; they were placed in an ambulance and brought to the commnad. These were placed with the advance guard of twenty men under Dick Yeager, who was appointed to pilot the command out. Before the horess had finished eating, the pickets fired; the order was given to mount and go west through a lane, the Federals getting closer all the time. At the mouth of the lane, Quantrell gave the command to form in line and, as the Federals came in sight, coming through a corn-field, he ordered a charge, the Federals running back a short distance. He again fell back and the Federals crowded right up. Some of the men becoming excited, broke ranks and rushed to the advance guard. Quantrell immediately formed his remainder in line and gave orders to shoot any man who attempted to pass. When the men had been quited and formed in line again, he said to them, "Now, if any of you intend to break ranks again, do it now; if you stay with me and act like men, I can get you out of this, but if you are going to run, go now, but do not come back to me." After this not a man broke ranks. The command then marched in line of battle all day, the Federals still following close and several times they started to charge, but when they would hear Quantrell give the command to about face, the Federals would always stop. Late in the evening, when within about fiive or six miles of the little town of Auberry, Yeager was seen to suddenly turn to the left. Quantrell remarked, "Boys, there's something wrong, or Dick Yeager would not have turned off." When the top of the ridge was reached, there was a regiment of Federals formed in line of battle. They stood in line until the entire command had passed, never offering to make a move or fire a shot. If they had made a charge while the other regiment was in the rear of

Quantrell and his command none of the command would ever have escaped. About ten o'clock at night, having reached a large pool of water, the command was given to unsaddle and to hold our horses by the bridles and let the meat grass and for none of us to go to sleep. Dick Barry and I sat down on our saddles and, not having closed our eyes for two days and two nights, we both dropped off to sleep and the next thing we heard was the command to saddle and mount. We sprang to our feet and our horses were both gone and, just at this time, we heard some of the boys say, "Here's a loose horse," I stayed with the saddles and Dick soon returned with our horses. We were soon mounted and rode all night long and, at sun rise, we reached the head of Grand River in Cass County, Missouri. From a ridge, we looked back into Kansas and the whole face of the earth was black with Federals following us. The two wounded men were then hid in the woods, but the Federals soon found them and killed them. We remained here and rested our horses until the Federals were within half a mile of us when we went across the prairie to Big Creek. Late in the evening, I saw some men to the right of the road in the edge of the timber. I told Quantrell that they were Federals and he said, "No, it's Andy Blount returning from Johnson county." I insisted that Blount did not have that many men with him, but he insisted that he was right and we moved right toward them. I remarked, "I reckon you can see their uniforms now and tell who they are," to which he replied, "If you are so darned certain of it, ride out and see." I started toward them in a gallop, two of them coming to meet me, firing at me. Quantrell then remarked, "That'll do, John; you are right. Come back." We then turned due east and they made a charge on us and, as we crossed a little ravine, they fired a volley at us, but struck none of us. In about a mile, having come to the Big Creek timber, Quantrell said "Disband and every man take care of himself."

CHAPTER XI.

I was truly glad when Colonel Quantrell gave the command because I was well acquainted in that country and wanted to get away from the command for it looked to me as if every bush had a Yankee behind it. I turned my horse into the brush about a hundred yards from the Federals and about forty of the boys started to follow me. I turned to them and said, "Boys, this'll never do; they can follow this bunch as well as they could the whole command, and they'll be on us in twenty minutes." As soon as we got to the creek we separated and seven of the boys went with me down the creek in the water about fifty yards and then coming out on the same side into the brush. Going about 100 yards into the brush, I told the boys to dismount and hold their horses by the bridles. We had hardly dismounted, when we saw the Federals going down the creek after the other boys and we soon heard some firing, but I do not think anyone was hurt. I was well acquainted with this locality and told the boys that I knew who lived there and, riding to the corn-field, some of the boys got corn and fed their horses while the others watched. I very cautiously went around toward the house and saw a man at the barn, feeding his stock. I gave him a signal and he came to the fence. As soon as he recognized me, he exclaimed, "Great God, John, haven't they got you yet?" I replied, "No, and they will not get me." "Yes,, they will," he said, "this country is full of them," to which I replied, "Well, if they do, while they are getting me, I'll get some of them." I then told him that we had not had a mouthful to eat for two days and two nights. He said he had plenty to eat, but nothing cooked, and for me to go into the woods and he would have his women cook us something to eat and he would bring it to us, but not to make any light. In a short time the old man came out and two of his girls with him, each carrying a bucket or a basket and one of them a large pot of coffee. After we had eaten our supper, I ordered the boys to saddle up, knowing that the Federals would be there next morning. We crossed the road leading from Pleasant Hill to Harrisonville and took a by-road leading through the fields, and, just before we came out on the main road, we heard the Federals crossing a bridge on Big Creek. They were coming directly towards us. We rode out into a corn field, dismounted and held our horses until they had passed. We then rode across the road into another cornfield and I told the boys to ride fast, which we did for about two miles and then went into the Big Creek bottom. At the lower end of the bottom, we crossed Big Creek at a cow ford. We then went into the woods, where we hitched our horses and, having been in the saddle for three days and three nights, without any sleep, we soon went to sleep and did not wake up until nine o'clock the next morning. That day we secured food from a neighborning house and, after dark, we rode out on the prairie where we could see the lights from two Federal camps about a mile apart. I told the boys that it would be dangerous for us to attempt to go either to the right or left of these camps and we decided to ride between and we were not even halted. We then went over on th Little Blue and stayed in the woods for several days.

About this time, there was issued by General Ewing, in command of the Federal troops at Kansas City, the famous Order No. 11, which was as follows:

Headquarters District of the Border,
Kansas City, Mo., August 25, 1863.

First: All persons living in Cass, Jackson and Bates Counties, Missouri, and in that part of Vernon County, included in this district, except those living within one mile of the city limits of Independence, Hickman's Mills, Pleasant Hill and Harrisonville, and except those in that part of Kaw Township, Jackson County, north of Brush Creek and west of the Big Blue, embracing Kansas City and Westport, are hereby ordered to move from their present places of residence within 15 days from the date hereof. Those who within that time establish their loyalty to the satisfaction of the commanding officer of the military station nearest their present place of residence, will receive from him certificates stating the facts of their loyalty and the names by whom it can be shown. All who receive such certificates will be permitted to remove to any military station in this district or to any part of the State of Kansas, except all the counties on the eastern border of the state. All others shall remain out of the district.

Officers commanding companies and detachments, serving in the counties named will see that this paragraph is promptly obeyed.

Second: All grain or hay in the fields or under shelter in

the district from which the inhabitants are required to move within reach of military stations, after the ninth day of September will be taken to such stations and turned over to the proper officers there; and report of the amount so turned over made to the district headquarters specifying the names of all loyal owners and the amount of such produce taken from them. All grain and hay found in such district after the ninth day of September next, not removed to such stations will be destroyed.

(Signed) H. Hannans, Adjutant, by order Brigadier-General Ewing.

The effect of this order meant utter ruin to all Southern citizens in this district. They were banished and robbed by the same order. No transportation was prepared for them. Their horses, mules and cattle had already been stolen and taken to Kansas along with their buggies, carriages and wagons, but fortunately it may be said, they did not have very much left to move.

In September 1863, Captain Bill Anderson again joined us and, after supplying ourselves with ammunition and clothing, we all started south again, there being about 150 men in both commands. We proceeded through southwest Missouri without meeting and Federals until we reached Carthage, in Jasper County. Having stopped near this town, we were awakened, just before day, by the noise of moving wagons. Colonel Quantrell immediately sent out scouts, who reported that there were a company of Federals moving north, and that they so greatly outnumbered us that we decided not to molest them. Going a little distance from this town, the boys brought into our camp two men claiming to be Southern men and Quantrell secured one of them a guide. About dark, we left camp and came to the road leading from Neosho to Fort Scott, on which we traveled until about 9 or 10 o'clock that night. Captain Todd rode up to me about that time and I asked him where Quantrell was going and he told me South. I then told him that we were going wrong and that our new-found guide was leading us to Fort Scott, Kansas, where there was a large force of Federals. I was well acquainted with this part of the country and knew what I was talking about. Quantrell sent for me and, after talking with him for awhile, he told me to take the lead and, if I did not show him the right way out of that country, he would shoot me. I told him to command the men to countermarch and, taking the lead with the advance guard, went back along the road for three miles and turning out of the road into a prairie, about 2 or 3 o'clock in the morning, we came to Reading's Mill on Shoal Creek in Newton County. Quantrell knew this place and, calling me to him, said, "John, you do know this country, and I will not have to shoot you. He then told me to go over to the mill and reconnoitre. I took Allen Palmer with me. We rapped on the door of the mill and one of the Redding boys came to the door and, recognizing me, asked me what I was doing there. I told him that I was with a command and wanted to know if there were any Federals in the country. He said none that he knew of nearer than Neosho, which was twelve miles distant. He told us to go up into his corn-field, hitch our horses and come back by the mill and get all the flour and bacon we wanted. The next morning we had a fine breakfast, bread made up of flour and water and twisted around a stick and cooked, broiled bacon and coffee. We then went from there to Fvie Mile Creek and there discovered a number of tracks of horses and Quantrell ordered us to follow them and when we reached the bottom south of the Neosho River we found ten or fifteen Federal soldiers guarding some wagons loaded with lumber going toward Baxter Springs. I sent word back to Colonel Quantrell and he came forward and ordered us to follow them. We captured the wagons as they were crossing the creek, the men on the horses dashing up the creek. Dave Poole took command of the advance guard of twenty men and followed the Federals, telling me to remain and inform Quantrell of the direction he had taken. We all then rushed up the creek and to our utter surprise, we found a fort at Baxter Springs. None of us had ever heard that there was a fort there with a command of troops stationed in it. While the boys were riding around trying to get a shot at the gunners in the fort, Quantrell himself discovered a company of Federals with a wagon train, ambulance and buggies, who were drawn up in line of battle on the prairie. We afterwards learned that this was General Blount's body guard of about two hundred men with nineteen wagons, four ambulances and five buggies and a brass band, that he had formed in line for the purpose of marching down to the fort at Baxter Springs and to have his band serenade them and take breakfast with them. Quantrell turned to me and told me to get the boys away from the fort and to form in line.

just as I had succeeded, the Federals fired from the fort with their two cannon, one of the balls litterally decapitating Dave Woods. Quantrell then rode behind the lines and when he had reached the center, rode out in front, taking off his hat, placed it in the bosom of his coat, touched his horse with his spur and said, "Come on, boys," and we started toward them in a run. When about seventy-five yards from the Federals we went into a little branch and then they fired on us, but did us no damage, none of our men even hearing a bullet whistle. We then went at them in our accustomed manner, yelling and shooting and they scattered across the prairie, running in all directions. There was an officer and a woman in a buggy, driving a very handsome pair of bay horses. Several of us boys tried to catch them and followed them about a mile and of course, we would not shoot at them on account of the woman. The woman was holding the lines and the man whipping the horses, and when they reached the main road, we decided to let them go and turned back on the prairie after the men. We really wanted the horses worse than we did the Colonel. We followed these soldiers for about three miles leaving most of them on the prairie and there were only a few of them that ever returned our fire. I galloped up to the side of a Federal officer, who had his revolver in his hand and commanded him to halt, but he only spurred his horse the harder. I snapped my pistol at him six times and discovered it was empty. I then struck him over the head with my pistol. He fell from his horse and I led his horse on with me. George Maddox caught up with a yellow negro driving General Blount's team. Blunt had left the buggy and mounted a horse and escaped when he first saw us. The team was an elegant pair of dun horses with docked tails. When Maddox first covered the negro with his pistol, the negro threw up his hands and said, "Before you shoot me, I want to ask you a question." Maddox told him to ask it damned quick. He then asked if Captain George Todd was in this command. Maddox told him he was and then the negro said, "Please don't shoot me until I see him." Maddox then took the negro up to where the wagon train was and told Captain Todd, and when Captain Todd had gotten within sixty feet of the negro, Todd exclaimed, "By God, it's Rube," and jumping off of his horse, ran up to him and shook hands with him and was as delighted to see him as if he had been a long-lost brother. Captain Todd then turned to the men and said, "Boys, the first man that hurts this nigger, I will kill." He then told us that during the winter of 1862, when he had returned from the South, where he had been with General Price and was visiting his wife, who was staying at his father's house in Kansas City, he was in the habit of going to a barber shop, which was run by Rube, who had for a number of years been known as a free negro. After Captain Todd had been in Kansas City several days, the Federal soldiers learned that he was there and determined to capture him and hang him, and some of them were discussing their plans in Rube's barber shop. As soon as Rube heard this, he immediately went to Captain Todd's father's house and informed him of the Federal plans, and told Captain Todd to wait until dark, then come to his house and go into the cellar. He stayed in this cellar for ten days, Rube feeding and taking care of him and keeping constantly on the lookout for the Federals, and one night assisted him in getting out of Kansas City. After Captain Todd had related to us these facts, none of the boys desired to harm Rube and we took him on South with us.

John Koger, one of our men, while busily engaged in examining the contents of a wagon, was shot from the fort, three buckshot and an ounce ball striking him in the back. It seemed that it was impossible to kill him, for at this time he already had in his body five Federal bullets, and fully recovered from these last wounds and lived until the fall of 1913.

Bill Bledsoe was riding by the Federal bandwagon when one of the members of the band fired on him, mortally wounding him. The driver of the bandwagon immediately forced his horses into a run. When Bledsoe fell from his horse, he said to Fletch Taylor, "Fletch, that outfit have shot and killed me; take my two pistols and kill all of them." Taylor immediately started in pursuit of the bandwagon and, in about a half a mile, one of the wheels came off of the bandwagon, throwing the occupants out, and Taylor dashed up to them and carried out Bledsoe's dying request, and then returned to Bledsoe and found him dead.

When I returned from chasing the Federals, I

met Colonel Quantrell coming from the wagon train, having in front of him, on his horse, a five-gallon demijohn of brandy that had been taken from General Blount's buggy. When he saw me, he said, in a very gruff manner, "John I thought you always knew that whenever a pilot led me into trouble, I always shoot him," and thinking that he was in earnest, I drew my revolver, remarking, "If you can shoot quicker than I can, shoot." He laughed and said, "Put that thing up, you damned fool; I'm going to shoot you in the neck," and handed me the demijohn of brandy. After shooting myself in the neck with the brandy, I rode up to a wagon that had already begun to burn and, seeing a small trunk in it, I threw it on the ground and breaking it open, I found it to contain a very handsome Federal colonel's uniform, a pair of fine cavalry boots, six white shirts and a pair of Colt's revolvers. Wrapping all of it except the revolvers in an oil-cloth, which I tied on the horse that I had taken fro ma Yankee, I rode on to another wagon where I found a fine saddle belonging to General Blount and I also found in the buggy General Blount's saber. I gave the saber and saddle to Colonel Quantrell and he afterwards presented the saber to General Sterling Price. General Blount was in the regular army, but when we examined his flag, which we captured here, we found sewed around the American eagle on the flag a border of black silk, which meant no quarter.

During this day we captured the notorious negro, Jack Mann, whose history we all well knew; having been raised in Jackson County, he was well acquainted with the locality and with all of the citizens and in 1861 he ran away from his owner and joined the Kansas redlegs and acted as their guide in a number of their murdering raids into Missouri. He was exceedingly insulting to the Southern people and especially so to the women and old men and, on one occasion, he led a squad of Kansas redlegs to the house of Dick Maddox, who was with us and, finding no one at home but Mrs. Maddox, this negro entered the house with his white associates and, cursing and abusing her all of the time. In ransacking the house, this black fiend found Maddox's wedding suit and, undressing before Mrs. Maddox, put the wedding suit on and, striding up before her, said, "How do you like my looks with this wedding suit on?" He had been guilty of a number of other similar offenses. When we captured him, Maddox, who was with us, wanted to shoot him at once, but Quantrell told him to wait, and that we would attend to his case later on.

After destroying this wagon train, we took an ambulance with four mules and let Rube, Captain Todd's pet nigger, drive his buggy. We put John Koger and Bill Bledsoe's corpse in the ambulance. When we had gone about ten miles, we stopped and buried Bill Bledsoe in an old cabin. While we were burying Bill, we left Will McGuire to guard the negro Jack Mann, who had made some insulting remarks to McGuire, who could stand it no longer and, drawing his revolver, shot him between the eyes. When Dick Maddox saw McGuire shoot the negro, he drew his revolver and started to shoot McGuire, because he had not let him shoot the black fiend. About sundown that evening, we came upon a wagon train of Pin Indians, who were supposed to be in the service of the Federal government and who, with the Kansas Jayhawkers, had killed and scalped a number of women and children. We charged on the Indians and, in a short time, they were all good Indians. Leaving this place, we marched until the next day when we came in sight of a camp of Pin Indians, containing 800 or a 1000 Indians and, knowing that they were too strong for us to attack while in camp, we went into camp near them, raising General Blount's flag in the hope that they would scatter and we could get at them. Captain Todd, while attempting to kill a beef, was hurt by his horse falling with him and he was placed in the ambulance for two or three days. We had no more real fighting for several days, occasionally "rounding up" a stray Indian and a stray nigger, and one morning, Bill Toller came across three armed negroes. They fired on him, shooting him through the arm, and he returned the fire, killing one of the negroes. We laughed at Bill a great deal about letting a nigger shoot him and get away. Having camped on a small stream, George Wigginton and I crossed a little branch and, taking the saddles from off our horses, were soon asleep. Quantrell not looking for any danger from the south, failed to place any pickets on that side of our camp and, just at daylight, we were awakened by the blast of a bugle, which was followed by a quick command from Colonel Quantrell, "Mount and form line." Wigginton and I sprank to our horses without taking time to sadle them and rode into line. Just then, a soldier rode in sight and yelled, "Don't fire boys; we are friends." We then learned that when the bugler sounded the charge their commander came to the ambulance where John Koger was and asked him who we were. He then told them who we were and not to fire, that if they did there would be five hundred men killed. When learning that we were Confderates, Colonel McIntosh, their commander, rode forward and we learned that it was a part of the famous Confederate Indian brigade, known as Cooper and Sandwadie's command, which was composed of Cherokee, Chickasaw and Choctaw Indians and a few white men. Colonel McIntosh had with him on this occasion 1,500 soldiers and had us ocmpletely surrounded. Their scouts had reported that we were coming that way and, as we were carrying General Blount's flag, wearing blue overcoats and having with us a Federal ambulance, it was very natural to mistake us for Federals. After talking awhile with Colonel Quantrell, Colonel McIntosh left pilots with us and invited us to come to their camp, which was about fifteen miles away. We soon started to their camp and were given a hearty welcome. The commander issued rations for us and our horses and we visited with them five or six days and then proceeded south across Red River to Sherman, Texas, where we remained two days and went into camp about two miles from the town of Sherman, where we remained for two weeks and then went into the neighborhood of Georgetown, on the south of Red River and remained in camp until the spring of 1864. During this winter, we spent our time hunting, fishing and going to dances and during Christmas week, quite a number of us attended a big ball in Sherman, having been invited by the young people of Sherman. We also received an invitation to visit General McCullough at Bonham, Texas. During Christmas week, Captain Bill Anderson married a Southern lady in Sherman, all of us attending the wedding.

CHAPTER XII.

On the 20th of March, 1864, we broke camp on Red River and started back north. Colonel Bard Cockrell, a brother of the fighting General Francis M. Cockerell, who for so many years, was United States Senator from Missouri, accompanied us. When we reached Cooper and Sandwadie's we stopped and stayed with them two days and Colonel McIntosh came with us as far north as the Canadian River. When we reached the Arkansas River, which was very high, after waiting two or three days for the water to run down and our provisions running short, Quantrell said we could wait no longer, but would have to swin it and as he was riding a good horse, he would cross first, but for not more than two of us to enter the river at once. He urged his horse into the river and reaching the other side in safety, he rode down to two log cabins and, finding two hogs in one of them, he fastened the door, riding back to the bank, he called to us "Hurry up, boys, I've got a good supper for you over here." When we had crossed, we killed the hogs, built a fire in the cabin and soon had burnt and scorched pork for supper. On the third day, after crossing the Arkansas River, we came to the log cabin where we had buried Bill Bledsoe. We found the cabin torn down and that wolves had eaten all the flesh from his body. We again reinterred his bones. Near this cabin, we also found the bare skull of the negro, Jack Mann, which we could identify by its thickness and a round hole in it. Here Colonel Quantrell told me to take the lead as I was well acquainted with the country from there on. We crossed the Neosho River at Gilstrap's ferry and, as we reached the edge of Buckhardt's prairie, we saw five men, who were Southern men and, mistaking us for Federals, they ran into the woods. Colonel Cockrell, who was wearing his Confederate uniform, said he would ride into the woods and talk to them, but they, still thinking that he was a Federal in disguise, fired on him, severly wouding him in the shoulder. We had neither feed for ourselves or our horses and Colonel Cockrell, who was very sore from his wound, said he could not ride and would have to stop. Quantrell told me that I would have to stay with him, which I very politely declined to do. He then said he would force me to stay, and I told him that as soon as he got out of sight, I would leave. Colonel Cockrell then decided that he could probably ride and we saddled his horse and he came on through with us. We reached South Grand River in Bates County and, learning that there was a company of Federals guarding the ford, we turned down the river and, reaching a point three miles below the ford at night, we made our horses swim the river. We stayed on the bank until morning. drying our blankets and clothes. When we came in sight of aDyton in Cass County, we saw some Federal soldiers there. We rode on and finally one of them rode out toward us. Will McGuire rode out to meet him and the Federal asked him what command we were. McGuire, drawing his revolver, told him we were Southern soldiers and he would have to go with us.

At this time, neither men or horses had had a mouthful of food for four days. We then reached a neighborhood where the Federals had left a few houses standing, where we succeeded in getting getting something to eat. I rode up to a lady's house and she told me that she could give me something to eat but had no feed for our horses and then she started in to frying ham and eggs, and I do not think that before or since in my life I have ever smelt anything as good as the ham and eggs did cooking. When we reached Johnson County, we learned that there were four hundred Federals at Chapel Hill. In passing a farmhouse, we saw two horses belonging to Federals officers. Two of the boys unhitched the horses, and left the officers unmolested. We started to go into the timber and when we were within about half a mile of it, the horses of Dave Hilton, George Wigginton, Nathan Carr and myself stopped and refused to go another step. They were too weak and poor to travel farther. Some of the boys road forward and told Quantrell and he came back and said it would not do to leave us there afoot. We took the saddles off of our horses and, leaving them on the prairie, we carried our saddles and blankets into the woods where we stayed all night. We stayed in the woods three or four days, Colonel Quantrell having left us and, at night we started out to find us something to eat and, after traveling for some time in the dark, we came to a house and I left the boys in the road and went to the door. After knocking several times, a lady raised the window and asked who was there. I asked how far it was to Chapel Hill and who lived there. She told me and I knew her husband. He came to the door and recognizing me, said he would look for something for us to eat, but he was afraid to strike a light. He soon returned with half of a boiled ham, a big loaf of home-made light-bread and a jar of buttermilk and in a very few minutes we had finished our lunch. He then gave us a large piece of dried beef each, telling us that that would keep us from starving. We would go to sleep walking along the road and, coming into a piece of timber, supposing ourselves well into the woods, we dropped down and went to sleep and did not wake up until 8 o'clock the next morning, when we found that we were within twenty or thirty feet of a public road. We then came out on the prairie and saw some houses we recognized and went to the house of the Widow Hill, the mother of Wood and Tuck Hill. We approached the house from the rear and Mrs. Hill came out on the porch and ran to us and told us to get away quick, that there were three hundred Federal soldiers camped in her pasture; there were five or six in her house at that time. We then went down the road leading to the Sni. By this time our supply of dried beef was exhausted and we stopped at a house on the edge of the timber and got something to eat and learned where some of the other boys were. The next morning, we went to Joe Hook's. Three of us were barefooted. At Mr. Hook's house, there were three young ladies, his two daughters and a Miss Wayman. Miss Wayman laughingly asked us what size boots we wore and told us to come back there the next night. We left and went from there to Dick Kinney's and found that he was also hiding in the woods. We stayed with Dick in the woods that night and the next night returned to Joe Hook's, where the young ladies presented us with a nice pair of boots and yarn socks each. They had been to Lexington that day and bought them. Being again among friends, we stayed in this neighborhood for ten or twelve days, always using the same bedroom at night—the woods. George Wigginton, Dave Hilton, George Langdon and I went down into Lafayette County and on down to Harlan on the Missouri River, where Hilton's mother, two sisters and little brother lived, her house having been burned in Jackson County, and she having been ordered to leave there by the militia. Dave remained with his mother and sisters and the rest of us went to John Wigginton's, near Waverly, his house also having been burned in Jackson County and he left under Order No 11. About this time George Langdon decided to go home, which was north of Rocheport in Boone County. We helped him secure a skiff and saw him start down the Missouri River. I afterwards saw him at his home after the fight at Centralia. George and I stayed at his father's, or rather, in the woods near there until the leaves were out again, and I went up to Joe Chrisman's, and he loaned me a good horse and bridle. George found him a horse and then we went on into Jackson County to find the boys. We were both riding bareback when we met Bill Yowell and he told us where we could find two good saddles hid in the woods. We found the saddles and we were ready for business again. Riding through Jackson County one night between the Sni and Tabo Creek, we rode right into a company of Federals who were asleep. We put spurs to our horses and dashed through. They opened fire on us and we could hear them firing after we were a mile away. We stayed around in Jackson County for several weeks, when we learned that Dave Poole was up on Tabo with about forty men. We joined them and then Dave decided to make another visit to his Dutch friends near Concordia. A short time before this some of the boys had captured a Federal flag, which we took with us, having a man to ride at our head, carrying it. When we had gotten within a quarter of a mile of the store, one of the militia saw us and recognizing Poole started to give the alarm. Some of our boys captured him and hung him to a stake on a rail fence. Poole rode up in front of the store and the old Dutchman, who owned the store, came out and seeing the Federal flag and taking us for Federal soldiers, exclaimed, "Oh, py golly, we sendt a company and now it is come already yet. Now, we get that tamned Davy Poole;

he's up on Tabo mit one leg broke. We take the company and go up in that Tabo brush and get him. He is vun tamned bad man; he come down here vun morning before breakfast und kicked me right before mine face and tell me my wife is vun bad woman." Dave Poole looked at him a minute and said, "Damn your Dutch soul, I'm Dave Poole that you're going after. Now, where's your money?" The old Dutchman threw up both hands, exclaiming, "I am vun of the bestest men you ever saw. I never done noddings wrong in all my life yet; I don't got some money." Poole replied, "Yes, you have, and get it quick. The fellow out here in the road told me you had money." "Who told you I had some money?" the Dutchman asked. Dave said, "Come out here and I'll show you," and, leading the Dutchman out in the road to where the man was tied to the fence-stake, he said, "That's the fellow that told me you had the money." The old Dutchman began to throw his hands around, exclaiming, "Oh, mine Gott, Mr. Poolie, my money's upstairs in my black britches pocket in a little rag tied up." While Poole was having fun with this Dutchman, the rest of the militia had gotten to the block house. We went back upon the Sni and about sixty of us met at an appointed place on the Sni, Captain George Todd being in command. Colonel Quantrell, soon after we had returned from the South, had taken with him Jim Little, John Barker, Tom Harris, Dave Hilton and Tom Evans, and, crossing the Missouri River at Arrow Rock, in Saline County, went into Howard

County, where he remained all summer until after Price's raid.

At this time there was stationed in Independence the Colorado troops, a regiment of Federal cavalry, who had made repeated threats that if ever they met us, they would exterminate our whole command. Captain Todd ordered us to go to a point on the Independence and Harrisonville road, where we cut the telegraph wires, taking several feet of it into the woods, knowing that this would bring the Federals out to hunt us. We went into the woods opposite the Widow Moore's place. In front of this place, and just across the road from where we were, there was an open field. We stationed pickets on the road and having waited until 2 o'clock, Captain Todd and Lee McMurty crossed the road, going up to Mrs. Moore's house and hitching their horses to the yard fence. Shortly after they had entered Mrs. Moore's house our pickets came in and told us that there were about twenty Federals coming and we supposed that this was all there were of them. As soon as they saw the two horses hitched to the fence, they started in a gallop. Todd and McMurty ran out, springing on their horses and started down the field, the Federals following them in the road. Lieutenant Dick Yeager ordered us to charge. We gained on the Federals and they left the road and went into the brush. Yeager then commanded us to dismount and follow them. Just as we had dismounted, we heard someone give the command, "Charge," and, looking back, we saw the rest of the Colorado company coming after us in a run. Yeager immediately commanded us to remount, about face and charge them. We rushed at them and threw them, wheeling our horses, we charged them again and in that open field this was repeated seven times, both commands wheeling and charging. This lasted until the Federals were out of ammunition and, to their credit it can be said that they were the bravest soldiers we had encountered. They had fought fearlessly and desperately till they had emptied their last pistol, but they shot too low, only wounding one of our men, but killing seven horses for us and wounding six of seven more. We killed thirty-seven of them and captured three of their horses. After the Federals had retreated one of the boys remarked to me, "John look at your hat," and taking my hat off I discovered a bullet hole through it and I also discovered two bullet holes through my coat under my left arm and one in front of my saddle. The only man we had wounded was Ike Flannery. He was shot under the right shoulder-blade, the ball passing through his body and tearing away his left nipple. Not having any physician with us, some of the boys took charge of him, keeping his wound well bathed with cold water and in thirteen days he had recovered and was ready to go with us again. We took a number of the pistols that the enemy were using which were a very large caliber pistol, known as the French Dragoon pistol and we then discovered why they had not killed more of us. These pistols were very heavy at the muzzle and would undershoot and none of our best marksmen could shoot them with any accuracy.

CHAPTER XIII.

In two weeks, we left our camp in Jackson County and rode to Arrow Rock in Saline County. There was a company of Federals stationed at Arrow Rock and as soon as they saw us approaching, they hastily departed from the town, going up the Missouri River. They fired back at us several times, wounding Dick Yeager. We secured a conveyance and took him up near Frankfort and kept him in the woods near the home of Ike Flannery's father, who was a refugee from Jackson County, and in about two weeks afterwards a company of Federal soldiers came down from Marshall and killed him. We returned to Jackson County from Arrow Rock and again went into hiding on the Sni and the Blue. At this time there were no people living on the farms in Jackson County, but near the towns there were a few Union men still on the farms. We found provisions hid in the woods that our friends had placed there for us. One night Captain Todd, Lee McMurtry, Bill Hulse, Allen Palmer, Payne Jones and I rode across to the East Blue and when we had reached the farm of an old man by the name of Shepherd, the Federals fired on us from ambush but the only damage they did was to shoot Lee McMurtry's horse through the nose. We returned the fire, but, on account of the darkness could not tell with what effect. We started to run when McMurtry's horse refused to follow us, but was plunging, snorting and blowing the blood from its nostrils. Lee yelled out, "Hold on, boys, my horse is shot." Some of us caught

MARY ANN WIGGINTON.

106B

his bridle rein and, riding around, we went back to where the remainder of the boys were.

On the 23rd day of August, 1864, John Mead, who was a new recruit, started with me to my uncle, John Wigginton's, to secure pistol caps that my cousin Mollie Wigginton had brought from Illinois.

Her brother, Will Wigginton, had been with General Price in the South and had been captured and placed in prison at Alton, Illinois. He and thirteen others had escaped from the prison by digging under the foundation with table knives. They would lie on their backs and dig, putting the dirt in their pockets and afterwards scattering it. Will worked in this position so long that he wore all the hair from the back of his head. They finally succeeded in escaping from Alton, being assisted by a guard. Will remained in the state of Illinois and wrote to his sister, Mollie, that he could furnish us with all the arms we might want. Mollie communicated this fact to me and I told her it was no trouble for us to secure all the arms we wanted from the Federals, but we did have trouble in getting pistol caps. Mollie immediately told her friends she had decided to make a visit to Illinois and was several days busily engaged in packing her trunk, in which she had a false bottom made. Leaving for Illinois and, taking her trunk with her, she visited Will and other relatives for about a week and when she returned to Missouri, there were 35,000 pistol caps between the two bottoms of her trunk. Uncle John, at this time, as had been said, was living in Lafayette County, Missouri. When Mead and I approached his house, we saw a command of Federal soldiers approaching and they had seen us. We wheeled our horses and started back through a hemp field, the Federals pursuing us. When we reached a ravine in the hemp-field, I told Mead to ride on and throw the riders off of the fence and I would stay and fire at the Federals and check them. After firing five or six shots, I dashed up to where Mead was and found him sitting on his horse trembling and never having touched the fence. I threw the rider off of the fence which my mare jumped and we then turned into the brush, when I stopped my horse and Mead began to yell to me, "Come on, for God's sake!" to which I replied, "In this kind of brush I am not afraid of the whole Federal army." The Federals then left us and returned to Uncle John's house and, calling him out, told him that they had been sent from Sedalia to kill him, knowing that he had a son with Quantrell and had been feeding and harboring the bushwhackers. They seized him and started out of the house with him. His aged wife and his daughter clung to him until they had reached the yard when the soldiers roughly jerked them back and riddled him with bullets, utterly ignoring the cries and pleas of the two women. This was another relative of mine whose foul murder I was called upon to revenge.

In three or four days, George Wigginton and I visited his mother and sister and, as we started to leave, we secured a number of the caps and, riding down into the hemp field, we found six negroes cutting hemp and, dismounting from my horse, I told one of the negroes to give me the cradle and let me show him how to cut hemp. Suddenly the two negroes looked up and said to me, "Young master, is dem some of your men coming yonder?" and I saw a company of Federals pursuing us. Not having any desire to longer cut hemp, I mounted my horse and we dashed through the field into the woods, the Federals firing at us, and Wigginton and I joined the other boys. In the latter part of August, 1864, sixty-eight of us went to a point between Independence and Wellington, and, crossing the Missouri River, the men going in skiffs and leading our horses, we entered Clay County. Going through Ray County and down through Carroll County on to Keytesville, the county seat of Chariton County. From Keytesville, we went south, crossing the east fork of the Chariton at Switzler's Mill into Howard County and going between the towns of Glasgow and Roanoke, we came to the Wilcoxson place, west of Fayette. During this entire march, we had traveled only at night. Procuring our breakfast at the Wilcoxson place, we went on into Boone County and, when about six miles from the town of Rocheport, on the Rocheport and Sturgeon road, at a point known as Goslin's Lane, we saw a train of about sixteen wagons with fifteen Federals in front and about sixty in the rear going in the direction of Rocheport. We dropped out of sight under a hill and, when about half of them had passed Gosline's house, we dashed on them and they divided, fleeing in utter confusion, going towards Fayette, Sturgeon, Rocheport and Columbia. I followed for quite a distance those going north and, being unable to capture any more of them, I returned to the wagon train, which was being burned. As I rode up to the wagon train, Dave Poole called to me, saying, "John, I just killed the damnedest longest yellow nigger I ever saw; he looks to me like he's nine feet long. Come and look at him." I went with him and saw lying near a wagon a negro with a blue uniform on and I agreed with Dave that he was the tallest man I had ever seen. In this little skirmish we killed twenty-five of the Federals without the loss of a single man.

We then turned back west into Howard County and, at the John R. White farm, between Franklin and Rocheport, we were joined by Captain Anderson and, in a few days, Captain Tom Todd and forty men, and Captain Thrailkill with sixteen men, joined us. And then to our delight, Colonel Quantrell, with his friends who had been with him in this county, came to us. The officers then held a consultation in regard to attacking Fayette. All were in favor of it except Quantrell, with whom Colonel Cale Perkins sided. He told the other officers there was no use in attacking men in brick houses and log cabins with only side arms; that if we did, we would only succeed in getting some of our men killed and wounded and we well knew that if any of our wounded boys fell into the hands of the Federals they would be murdered and insisted that we let Fayette alone and the facts afterwards demonstrated that Quantrell was right, but the majority of the officers being against him, on the 24th of September, we started for Fayette. Here was a command of Federals under Colonel Reeves Leonard, who were fortified in the courthouse and the college building and on a hill southwest of the college. They had fortifications built of logs. When we reached the creek southeast of town, we halted and John B. Dickerson, who now lives in the town of Fayette, and for a number of years has been City Marshal, was asked to take the lead and pilot us through the town, but John demurred, saying that his father and mother were living in Fayette and that the Federals would burn their home and murder his father and he recommended that Captain Tom Todd, who was also well acquainted with the town, take the lead. Captain Todd, taking the lead, the command, "Forward, march" was given and we dashed into the town up the street leading from the graveyard to the courthouse square and when we reached the corner of the square, we turned west one block, then turned south a block, then back again, all of us riding at the top of our speed and were passing down a side street when the Federals from the court house poured a perfect volley into us. On of these bullets struck Lee McMurtry under the left eye, giving him a severe flesh wound, blinding him for the time being and he fell from his horse. I caught his horse, led it back to him and, assisting him to mount, I led his horse down a side street to a pasture near where the Fayette High School is now situated. The remainder of our command went on up the street leading toward the town of Glasgow where the Federals had log fortifications. When I reached the pasture I there found Colonel Quantrell with Jim Little, who had received a bad wound in the right arm. I left McMurtry with

Quantrell and started up north for the town where I could hear a great deal of firing. Quantrell called to me and asked me where I was going, to which I replied, "To help the boys." He said, "Come on back, there's no use trying to shoot through brick walls and logs with pistols." I then turned my horse and rode back to where he was. In a few moments the rest of the command came back, having failed to dislodge the Federals and only killing four of them. We had five men killed and several severely wounded. One of our best men, Ol Johnson was shot through the hips. We placed him on a pillow on a saddle and led his horse six or eight miles from Fayette in the neighborhood of Washington Church and placed him in the woods near the farm of Jeff Payne and Mr. Payne's two daughters, Miss Pollie, now the widow of A. J. Kirby, a Confederate soldier and her sister, Miss Letitia, now the widow of Robert Baskett, carried him food and water and that splendid Southern gentleman, the late Dr. W. C. Harvey, of Roanoke, at the risk of his own life, visited him daily. Ol only lived five days and, just before he died, the doctor having told him that there was no hope for him, he wrote a long letter to his mother, who was at that time living in Jackson County, and Dr. Harvey sent it to her.

Quantrell left us at Fayette, going back into Boon's Lick Township and taking Jim Little with him. The rest of us went up towards Roanoke, some of us passing through the town, and that night we camped on Silver Creek near Mt. Airy.

The next day we passed within a few miles of

CAPTAIN BILL ANDERSON.

112b

Huntsville where there was a company of Federals. Captain Anderson wanted to go in and attack them, but Captain Todd, who was in command, refused, saying he had enough experience in trying to shoot through brick walls with pistols. That night we camped near Renick and the next day we went into the woods southeast of Centralia in Boone County.

Captain Anderson wanted us to go into the town of Centralia, but Todd refused to do it, so Anderson took his own company, leaving us in the woods and went into the town. While he was there a passenger train came in on the North Missouri Railroad, which is now the Wabash, with a number of Federal soldiers aboard. Anderson had all the passengers and soldiers get out on the platform and, separating the soldiers from the other passengers, he and his men shot and killed all the Federal soldiers. He then commanded the engineer to start his train, having set fire to the coaches. The old engineer, James Clark, who died a few years ago at Moberly, Missouri, when he started his engine, opened a valve, so that the water would soon run out of the boiler and the burning train soon stopped after only running a few miles. Captain Todd nor none of our command were with Anderson at the time and knew nothing of the killing of the soldiers until Anderson returned to our camp and told us, when Captain Todd severely reprimanded Anderson for doing it, telling him that he did not indorse such actions.

In the afternoon, our pickets came in and reported that there was a command of Federals coming with a black flag hoisted. Captain Todd ordered

Dave Poole to go and see who they were. He returned and reported that there were between two and three hundred of them. Todd then commanded us to form in line, telling us that he would ride ahead of us and for us to remain standing until he signaled us to come forward. He took three men with him, leaving us behind the brow of the hill out of sight and when the Federals had gotten to the foot of the hill, he raised his hat and we loped to him.

Major Johnson was in command of the Federals and, while in Centralia, he was bragging how he was going to extinguish our entire command, showing his black flag and saying that he would take no prisoners, but would kill us all. The citizens begged him not to go, but he only laughed and told them that it would be no more to him than a breakfast party and when he was starting a lady came out to his horse and, taking hold of his bridle rein, asked him not to go, telling him that George Todd and Bill Anderson were both there. He told her to stand aside, that he would kill us all and for her to watch for him when he returned, that he would have Todd's and Anderson's heads tied to a pole.

When we reached Captain Todd after he had signalled to us he commanded us to dismount and tighten our girths. When we dismounted, the Federals yelled, "They are dismounting; they are going to fight us afoot." Johnson then gave the command for his men to dismount and every fourth man to hold horses. We stood by our horses until their horses had been led away, when Captain Todd said, "Remount. Charge and kill them." We sprang into our saddles and started after them, each one of us trying to get there first. They fired one volley and then, becoming utterly demoralized, stampeded in all directions, some of them running for their horses and some of them starting for Centralia afoot. We followed them into the town of Centralia, which was about three miles away, dealing death at every jump. Some of them went through the town of Centralia and Frank James, Bill Hulse, Pink Gibson, Lee McMurtry, three others whose names I have forgotten and myself followed them to the edge of the town of Sturgeon, when we saw the Federal infantry stationed there forming into line to come out to meet us. Frank James then said, "Hold on, boys, we've killed enough of them; let's go back." When we turned to start back, I found my mare could not go out of a walk, I having run her for nearly eleven miles. Frank James said "That's all right, John; we'll not leave you and, if necessary we'll take you behind one of us." Pink Gibson, whose horse was comparatively fresh, galloped ahead of us and told Captain Todd, who sent me another horse.

There were 206 men in Major Johnson's command when we met them, and there were fourteen of them escaped, 2 of the latter number were badly wounded. We had one man killed, Frank Shepherd, who was shot in the head when they first fired. He was riding between Frank James and I when he was shot and the blood from his wound spurted on Frank's boot. Dick Kinney was shot through the knee and afterwards died from his wound.

When we had gotten back to our camp we only

stayed a short time, going in a southeast direction to Big Cedar Creek in Boone County. We rode seven or eight miles and scattered, trying to find something to eat. We then secured a pilot, who said he knew the country well and could take us out of it. We turned west and crossed a big creek. It was dark as pitch and raining torrents and our pilot became lost. Captain Todd then commanded us to dismount and every man get under a tree and stay until daylight. When daylight came we went up to a cornfield and were getting corn to feed our horses, and hearing someone on the other side of the field, we sent a man to find out who it was and he returned and told us that it was General Guitar with his entire command of Federals getting corn for their horses. Captain Todd then said, "Boys, this country's full of Federals and they are all after us and we'll have to disband and scatter." He told me to get my squad together and start. I said, "Captain, I know nothing about this country and I do not know a man in it." He replied, "You know as much about it as I do, and you have never been any place yet that you've failed to get out of, so take your men and go ahead." I called my men together and rode through the woods all day and, just at sun-down, I rode up to a house and asked if we could get something to eat and feed for our horses. He told us that we could but we would have to wait until supper was cooked. He started to the barn with us, and looking back, asked, "Are they some of your men coming too?" I told him I thought not, that they were Federals probably. He then told us to ride through his yard and into a field and they could not see us. Crossing a field, we came out into a narrow lane and I saw two men in the road. I called to them to halt, which they did and I asked who they were and they told me citizens and one of them very promptly said, "We don't know who you are, but we are both Southern men." I then asked them where they lived and they told me about half a mile from where we were and invited us to go home and take supper with them. After supper one of the men and two of my men went over to where the Federals had run us from and came back and reported that there was a company of Federals camped in the yard. We stayed in the woods that night and, leaving early the next morning, we rode until late in the afternoon when we came to Goslin's Lane where we had had the fight shortly before. This was the first place I recognized. We rode up to a house and found two ladies at home. One of them asked me if we were in the fight that had taken place there shortly before. I told her "Yes." She then asked me if any of us had lost part of a pistol in that fight. Jim Younger told her that he had lost the cylinder of his pistol and the lady remarked, "Well, we found some part of a pistol out there in the road; I don't know what you call it, but here it is," and it was the cylinder of Jim Younger's pistol that he had lost in the road pursuing some of the Federals.

The next morning we met one of Captain Anderson's men, John Holt, and we stayed with him that day and that night we went up to near Boonesboro in Howard County and found Colonel Quantrell and several of the other boys.

While we had been with Todd, Colonel Quantrell had remained near Boonesboro and while there a Captain Kimsey came to him with seven or eight men, claiming to be Southern soldiers and told it around the country that he had joined our command. He would go to citizens in this neighborhood, there being quite a number here who were refugees from Jackson County, and would tell them that Quantrell was waiting for Captain Todd's return with the men and had told him to secure money and horses from Southern friends. Captain Kimsey became very insulting in his demands for money and horses and some of the citizens went to Colonel Quantrell and complained of Kimsey's manner. He was utterly surprised, telling his friends that he had never authorized Kimsey nor anyone else to get money or horses from Southern citizens and that he would investigate it. He immediately mounted his horse and, taking several of the boys with him, he found Kimsey and told him he wanted to see him about robbing Southern people and telling that he had instructed him to do it and to consider himself under arrest and to turn over his revolver. Kimsey drew his revolver, telling Quantrell he had no authority to arrest him and attempted to shoot, but was too slow, Quantrell killing him.

CHAPTER XIV.

After staying in this neighborhood for a few days, Quantrell told us that Jim Little was not well enough to leave and for us to go on to a place near

Rocheport, where it had been prearranged we should meet, and to tell Captain Todd to take command and for us to ask to go south and spend the winter. When we met Captain Todd at the appointed place, there were with him Captain Anderson, Captain Thrailkill and Captain Tom Todd, having in all about 240 men, and Captain George Todd assumed command. We then went to the Missouri River, and, having secured skiffs, we began to cross the river. We would get into the skiffs, take a horse that was used to swimming by the bridle and then tying a horse to the tail of a horse ahead of him, start across the river, making the horses swim behind us and in this manner I crossed sixty horses at one time. We rested our horses a while, drying them the best we could and started on south through Cooper County. After going about two miles from the river, we saw two horses hitched in front of a house. George Shepherd and I asked permission of Captain Todd to go and see who they belonged to. He consented, but told us to be very careful as the county was full of Dutch militia. When we got to the horses, we saw they had fine new saddles and bridles and blue overcoats tied behind each saddle. We went into the house and an old Dutchman and his wife met us. We asked them who was in the house and they would talk nothing but Dutch. Both of them were wearing wooden shoes. We then left, untying the two horses and taking them with us and, after riding a short distance in the road, we saw a dead militiaman lying in the road. Shepherd remarked, "Hell's to pay, John, we'd better ride fast," and every few yards, we would find a dead militiaman lying by the side of the road. In about three miles, we soon discovered that our command had left the road and had turned into a cornfield. Just after making the turn around the cornfield we met a man in citizen's clothes and, taking him with us, we went on until we found our men in camp and our prisoner turned out to be a Southern man who was going South to join Price. The boys told us that while Shepherd and I were after the two horses they had suddenly met a company of militia, who immediately wheeled and fled, our boys following them and had killed over half of them.

The next morning we went on to Sedalia in Pettis County, and then to Sweet Springs, Saline County. When we entered Sweet Springs we scattered to get our breakfasts. I rode up to a house and asked a lady if I could get something for my horse and myself to eat. She told me the barn had plenty of feed in it and she would prepare me some breakfast. Just then Dave Poole rode up, remarking he was hungry too. She invited us both in and told us to wait a minute. She then asked us if we ever indulged in anything stronger than water to drink. We told her we did. She then took us into the dining room, seated us at the table and procured a quart bottle of whisky, and told us to fix a toddy to suit ourselves. We ate a hearty breakfast and as we were leaving, she insisted on my taking a bottle of whisky, remarking that her husband was with Price and she wouldhave another bottle for him when he returned home. I took the bottle and put it in my pocket and Dave remarked that he had been detailed to ride in front and would insist on my riding with him, especially as long as the whisky lasted.

When we started from Sweet Springs, it was decided that we should go up into the Dutch settlement near Concordia, David Poole being very anxious to again meet his old friends. Just before reaching the town of Concordia, we came to a place in the road, to the right of which was a field of corn in the shock and on the left a very dense brush thicket. Just as our advance guard, consisting of twenty men, under command of Dave Poole, and who were at least a mile ahead of the rest of the command, got opposite the brush, we were fired on from the brush, but none of us were hit. Poole told the boys to scatter around the thicket as well as they could and me to go back and tell Captain Todd to come on, that the Dutch were in the thicket. I dashed back, informed Captain Todd; he came up on the double quick, ordering the men to surround the thicket and for some of them to go in and run them out. What occurred afterwards reminded me of a rabbit hunt in the country. The boys started in the brush and every few minutes out would run a Dutchman and the boys on the outside would start after him. Not one of them escaped. Our advance guard then started on towards Concordia, when we discovered over two hundred Dutch coming toward us. The rest of the command hurriedly came and formed in line just over the brow of the ridge and, as the Dutch militia came over the hill, Todd ordered us to charge and kill them. We made a dash toward them and they made a dash to get away. We ran them into a lane, some of them left their horses and, running over into a corn field, they would hide in the shocks, where our boys would soon find them and get them out. There were very few of this company that ever reached home alive.

We went on up into the western portion of Lafayette County and the eastern portion of Jackson county. Here Captain Anderson and his company left us and came on down into Howard County. This was the last time I ever saw Bill Anderson and the next I heard of him he had been killed. We then scattered out, Captain Todd telling us to meet the gang at Bone Hill and wait until General Price had reached that part of the country when we all would join him.

One night, while we were waiting, Captain Todd was with me and several of the other boys in the brush. We were all discussing Price's return into Missouri and what effect it would have, when Captain Todd, who seemed that night more serious than usual, remarked, "Boys, when Price gets here, I will join him and, in the first battle I am in with him, I shall be killed and I want you boys to see that I have a decent burial." I remarked, "Well, Captain, if I thought I was going to be killed I would not go into the battle." He said, "Yes, I am going and I want you boys to go with me. I know I'll be killed, but it is just as fitting for me to die for my country as any other man. All I ask is that you boys stay with me and see that I get a decent burial."

In a few days Price had gotten near where we were and had been constantly engaged with the enemy. I waited until the time set by Captain Todd to meet at Bone Hill and when I reached there, I found that he had left and had left word for me to go to Captain Hedgepeth's on the Six Mile Prairie and to wait until he came back. I waited until evening and then went into the woods and stayed. The next morning, with the men I had with me, which were about thirty, I started out to find Captain Todd, when I soon met Dan Vaughan. As soon as I saw Dan I knew there was something serious the matter and when he came up to me he said, "John, Captain Todd wants you. He was badly wounded yesterday near Blue Mills and told me to come and find you and for you to come to Independence and bring the boys with you, that he wanted to see you all before he died." We started for Independence, having taken a circuitous route to avoid the Federals and, within about three miles of the town, we met General Fagan, going out to engage the Federals. He wanted us to stop and go with him, but I said, "General, the other boys may stay if they want to, but George Todd is wounded and thinks he's dying and has sent for me and I'm going to see him." I then hurried on towards Independence, and just as I entered the town I saw the boys coming out with Dave Poole in command. As soon as Dave saw me, he dropped his head and I knew it was all over. He rode up to me, and extending his hand, his eyes filled with tears, and he said, "John, our brave leader is gone. We are just returning from burying him. I am sorry you were not with him, for during the night he called for you frequently, and once in his delirium, he said, 'Boys, we're in a tight place; where is John McCorkle? If he was here he could get us out of this.'" The entire company then uncovered and, after a few minutes, I suggested that we elect another leader and proposed Dave Poole. He, at first, declined and suggested Henry Porter, but the boys insisted on his taking it and he remarked, "Well, if you boys insist, I will act, but I want it understood now that you boys must obey orders." I then asked permission of Captain Poole to stay a day or two and visit some friends and six of us remained and Dave went on.

I stayed in Independence about an hour, spending most of my time at the newly made grave of George Todd, whom I loved better than a brother, and started to the country to see if I could find any of my old friends, when I met Captain Beebe, one of General Price's officers, who, with his command, was formed in line of battle just southeast of Independence. He asked me to what command I belonged and when I told him, he said, "Then you know this country. I want you to go out and see what the Federals are doing and report to me at once." It did not take us boys long to see that the Federals were coming in town and I reported to him that they were getting ready to attack Price's rear guard. He immediately took his command and left town. Just then, I noticed a man whom I took to be a Confederate officer riding down a lane and, asking him who he was, he informed me he was Colonel Elliott and was trying to locate the Federals. I immediately informed the Colonel that it was no trouble to locate the Federals as they were already in town and the best thing for him to do was to get out of that lane and to join me. He then asked me if I could get him out of that and I told him I could but that we would have to ride lively. We then took the road toward Harrisonville and found a squad of forty pickets that had never been relieved. Colonel Elliott told them to come with us and, going about three quarters of a mile, we saw some Federals advancing. We exchanged fire with them, they following us for about a mile and, as we crossed a ridge, I suggested to Colonel Elliott that we had better form in line and fire them a volley, which we did, checking them. I then rode ahead and, meeting an officer, I asked him where he belonged and he asked me what company was with me and I replied, "Most anybody's," "but who is your commander?" he replied. "I belong to Colonel Elliott's battalion." I then told him that Colonel Elliott was with us and that I was one of Quantrell's men. He then turned to his men and exclaimed, "Boys, here's our Colonel. He is safe," and the entire command began to shout, for they thought their colonel was either dead or captured. When we reached Colonel Elliott's battalion, we found Dave Poole with them. We finished that day south of Westport, fighting with the Colorado troops, without the loss of any of our men.

We then went into camp and went to bed without any supper, our horses having feed and we nothing. The next morning for breakfast, we had a little raw beef and before we had time to even burn it over the coals, we were again ordered to the front. We were placed on a ridge with General Shelby to our left and with the understanding that General Marmaduke was to our right. About ten o'clock, still acting as courier and pilot, I rode out a little distance from our battalion and noticed a command moving toward us. I immediately rode back and told Colonel Elliott and Captain Poole that the Federals were approaching us from the right. They said I was mistaken, that it was General Marmaduke's command. I told them that Marmaduke's men did not wear blue clothes. Captain Poole then told me if I was so certain that they were Federals to ride out and see. I started toward them; two men left their command and came to meet me. I asked them who they were and they said Union soldiers; they asked me what command I belonged to and I told them Elliott's battalion of the Confederate cavalry and they both shot at me. I wheeled my horse and dashed back and told Colonel Elliott and Poole that I was going to General Shelby, that maybe he could tell a Yankee from a Confederate. Shelby rode up and taking in the situation, ordered Colonel Elliott to hold his position until he saw Shelby coming with his command. When we saw Shelby advancing we moved forward at the double quick, the Federals keeping pace with us and were about to cut us off when some of Price's infantry, who had hidden behind a rail fence, fired on them and checked them. In this advance the Federals captured seven of Shelby's men and promptly shot them. We crossed Big Blue, dark having come on us, when we went into camp and just after dark, the courier from General Price came and handed Captain Poole a note, which was a request from General Price that he take his men and leave the army because the Union soldiers were

MRS. LIZZIE GREGG.

126b

shooting Shelby's men that they had taken prisoners on account of hearing that Quantrell's men were with Shelby. Captain Poole sent work back to General Price, telling him that we would leave immediately. He then gave command for us to mount and we left the army, passing in safety between two Federal camps and riding on until we were in the edge of Johnson County and from there, we formed two camps, one on Tabo Creek and one on the Sni, where we made preparations to go south.

While we were in camp on the Sni, Bill Gregg told me that he was going to marry a beautiful Southern girl, Miss Lizzie Hook, and take her south with him and wanted me and some of the boys to go to the wedding with him. After dark, Gregg put on a new uniform and twelve of us put on our best and polished our pistols and spurs and accompanied him to the home of the bride. It was a strange scene, that wedding ceremony, a beautiful black-eyed, black-haired Southern girl, with her little hand placed on the arm of a stalwart soldier with four Navy revolvers buckled around his waist and with twelve long-haired, heavily-armed soldiers standing as witnesses and with only the members of the family beside the soldiers present, she plighted her young life to this grim warrior, fully realizing that at any moment she might be a widow, but this was only one example of the love of a Southern girl. We all stayed to a fine supper and we twelve, at a late hour, left the house and stood as guards for the bride and groom until we were called to breakfast the next morning. We then separated and went back on Tabo, some of us waiting until Quantrell could join us and the remainder of the boys, not wanting to wait for Quantrell, elected George Shepherd commander and started South at once. I saw them leave, Bill Gregg, with his bride by him, starting with us. Gregg and his wife made the journey South with the boys and are both living today in Kansas City, Missouri.

In a few days after Captain Shepherd and his men left, Colonel Quantrell returned and we started South. He told us that he intended to cross the Missouri River at Arrow Rock, go across the State of Missouri into Illinois, then into Kentucky and thence into Virginia, that we were all to wear Federal uniforms and to pass ourselves as Union soldiers, and his name was to be Colonel Clark, in command of a Colorado regiment. When we reached the Missouri River we found it so full of ice that we could not cross. Quantrell left us there and returned to Lafayette County, and after waiting several days, we started back to Lafayette County to join Quantrell again. We reached a farm on a high mound in Saline County and asked the owner if there were any Federals around. He said none nearer than Marshall and, as from his house we could see the country in every direction for miles, we decided to stay there all day and about ten o'clock a big flock of wild geese settled among the corn shocks in front of the house. Tom Harris and I went down into the field and killed five geese with our revolvers and the lady cooked them for our supper. We then rode from there on and when near Grand Pass Lake, Jim Lilly and

I killed a deer. We got down and cut its throat and quartered it, each man taking some and tying it to his saddle. I rolled the hide up and tied it to my saddle. When we reached the edge of Lafayette County and rode up to the house of Baltimore Thomas and when I called him out, I told him that I had come to bring him a piece of venison and presented him with the hind quarter and the hide. He said he would have the hide tanned and have us a pair of gloves made out of it. In 1865 I returned to Waverly on a visit and, meeting Mr. Thomas, he presented me with a very handsome pair of gloves that he had had made out of the hide.

We joined Colonel Quantrell near Dover and started on south, going through Lafayette, Saline, Cooper, Moniteau and into Miller County, the weather being extremely cold. At Tuscumbia on the Osage River, there was stationed a company of militia and we, wearing Federal uniforms, all rode into the town and right up to their headquarters without being molested. Quantrell asked for the commander and as he appeared, saluted him, telling him that we were out on a scout and would like to have feed for our horses and as we were all very cold we would like to warm. The commander had a fire built in their headquarters and invited us in. The Federals were standing around the room and we circled between them and the fire and also got between them and their arms, which were stacked in the corner of the room and, when we heard Quantrell, who had remained on the outside with the commander, tell him to surrender, we drew our revolvers and told the Federals that they were mistakn in their men, that we were Confederate soldiers and they were under arrest. They all promptly obeyed, except one man, who attempted to get out of a window, when Frank James gently tapped him on the head with his pistol and told him to get back in line or he might be seriously hurt. We marched the militia out into the street and, placing a guard over them, the rest of us proceeded to take their guns, break the stocks off of them and throw them into the river. Seeing us do this, one of the militiamen exclaimed, "Why, what in the world are they throwing our guns into the river for; we are Union men as well as they are?" to which his commander replied, "Why, you damned fool, they are Southern men and we are all prisoners." They had just received a new supply of blankets and clothing to which we helped ourselves. There was a ferry on the Osage River, consisting of an old flat-boat and an old over-head rope pulley. We compelled some of them to ferry us and our horses over the river and just before the last load crossed, Colonel Quantrell administered an oath to the soldiers that they would never again take up arms against the Southern Confederacy and told them to go and when he had crossed, we cut holes in the bottom of the boat and it sunk. We never fired a shot nor hurt a man.

We took two of these militia along with us to act as pilots and kept them for three days, when they informed us that they had reached a country with which they were unfamiliar and that it would be no use for them to continue further with us, when we paroled them, instructing them not to report to any command for two days.

We then proceeded southeast until we reached the Current River, which we followed into Arkansas. After we had gotten into the state of Arkansas, Joe Hall was taken with the small pox, and leaving Ike Hall, his brother, with him as a nurse, we left them near the town of Pocahontas, Arkansas. We then crossed the Black River and started through the swamps to Crawley's Ridge. We stopped about halfway through the swamps at a large house built of cypress logs and on this place, there was also a very large smokehouse and barn. A lady came to the door and told the Colonel that they had nothing to eat whatever. I was very doubtful as to the veracity of this statement and, being rather hungry, I went behind the smokehouse and removed a board and discovered that it was nearly full of flour and bacon. I told the Colonel that the lady was evidently mistaken and he demanded the keys, telling her that she had probably forgotten what her smoke-house contained and we helped ourselves to a sack of flour and some bacon. We camped in the barn lot and about nine o'clock that night, I discovered a fire in the woods and calling the Colonel's attention to it, he detailed me to take three of the boys with me and investigate. Entering the woods, we discovered that it was a light from a lamp in a house. I told the boys to watch and I would go to the house, but not to fire a shot unless they were forced to. Riding up to the door, I called, which created quite a commotion in the house and two men ran out of the back door into the woods. An old gentleman came to the door, asking who was there. I told him "a friend" and to come on out. I told him that we were Southern men and asked him who the men were that ran out of the back door. He said they were his two boys, who were at home on a furlough from the Southern army. I told him to call them back. He whistled a few times and the two boys came in. I then asked about the man that lived where we were camped. They told me he was a captain of what was called the Mountain Boomers, who did no fighting, but robbed and plundered both sides. I took the two boys back to camp with us, keeping out of sight of the people at the house, and they imparted to Colonel Quantrell some very valuable information, especially about the gentleman who lived in the big house, telling us that the great quantity of provisions that he had stored in his smoke-house had been stolen from the citizens in that part of the country.

When we left the next morning, we helped ourselves to the gentleman's provisions, knowing that he had stolen them. We went on until we had reached Crawley's Ridge, riding down the ridge until we came to the plantation of Colonel Morrison. Here Jesse James, John Koger, Ben Morrow, Baker Hedgpeth, Rufus Hedgpeth and Bob Hedgpeth left us and went on South to the army.

Still passing ourselves off as Union soldiers, we rode to the banks of the Mississippi River opposite Memphis, where we tried to make arrangements to cross the river. Being unable to get across the river at Memphis, we went twenty-five miles up the river to a little place called Shawnee Village, on Devil's Bend. We dismounted and leaving our horses in the brush, drew up in line on the river bank. We had not waited long before we saw a Federal transport coming up the river. Quantrell hailed it and, telling the Captain that we were a scouting party from Memphis, which had been cut off by the rebels, asked him to cross us. The captain told him he had strict orders not to land at that bank any more, that General Joe Shelby had slipped in there and captured two of their transports and sunk them.

The next day, we found a man by the name of Murray Boswell, who had formerly lived in Lafayette county, Missouri, who had an old yawl hid in the swamps. We got it out and repaired it with old lumber and nails that we could get from the houses and fences. We worked at this until New Year's Day, 1865, and all we had for our New Year's dinner was bread, made from wheat that we ground in handmills ourselves, which we cooked, bran and all, as we had no sifters.

Having fixed the yawl, at dusk Allen Palmer and I made the first trip, he leading two horses and I leading four. While we were crossing, a Federal transport came in sight. We held the yawl in some willows until it had rounded the bend. It took us all night to cross the command, there being forty-seven of us in all and we were told that at the point where we crossed the river was seven miles wide. After staying on the bank until we had gotten our horses dry and warm, we went on East for about a mile and, coming to a fine Southern plantation, with a beautiful blue grass pasture in front, we asked permission of its owner to camp there. He treated us in a very friendly manner and sent us food from his home. About nine o'clock the next morning, a man in his shirt sleeves, but with blue pants and a heavy revolver on and asked for our commander. When he met Colonel Quantrell he immediately became very confidential and told him that the owner of that plantation was an outrageous rebel, doing all in his power for the South and that he hoped that we would kill him before we left. Quantrell told him all right to stay there with his men awhile and he would go up to the house and interview this old rebel. Leaving our visitor to be entertained by us he mounted his horse and went up to the house. He was invited in by the proprietor and, after being seated, told him that he was Colonel Quantrell and was taking his command through to Virginia and also told him what our visitor had said about him. The proprietor then told Quantrell that our visitor, while a native of that country, was a Federal spy and was constantly watching and getting the Southern citizens into trouble and if any of the Southern soldiers returned, this man would promptly report it to the authorities at Memphis, and they would be arrested or killed. Quantrell bid our host goodbye, thanking him for his hospitality toward us, and returned to the camp, ordered us to saddle up and mount. He then turned to our visitor, ordered him to give up his revolver and took him with us. The next report that this traitor made was to Him who receives final reports from us all.

We went on towards the Kentucky line. In a few days, we were joined by a Federal soldier, who lived in that country, who made himself exceedingly familiar, riding with Colonel Quantrell nearly all day and pointing out to him the homes of rebels, telling him which ones ought to be killed and which houses ought to be burned. Just about dusk, he pointed to a certain house, saying, "That rebel that lives there ought not to be permitted to live another day. He is rich and the worst rebel in this country and has done more to aid the damned rebels than any man in the country." Quantrell turned to John Barker and told him to take this man with him and go up there and attend to that rebel. John left with our informant and in an hour returned alone, and the rebel who lived on the hill was not molested; the man who talked about him never talked about his neighbors any more.

CHAPTER XV.

Just before we reached the Kentucky line we learned that at a little town in Tennessee, there was a command of Confederates under Colonel Robert Fristoe, who was my uncle. Uncle Robert had lost his right leg at the battle of Franklin, Tennessee, but was still in the Confederate army. He had received word that there was a company of Missourians coming and, just before we reached the town, a lady rode up on horseback and asked Colonel Quantrell if we were Missourians and if there were any Fristoes with him, saying that she was the wife of Colonel

Fristoe. He told her that there were no Fristoes with him, but there were three of her husband's nephews, Tom Harris, George Wigginton and John McCorkle. He sent back for us and we came forward and were introduced to her, none of us ever having seen her before. She asked permission for us to go to town with her and we did so, reaching the town some time before the command and were heartily greeted by our uncle, who wanted us to stay with him, but we refused to leave the other boys and, after staying with Uncle about two hours, we crossed into Kentucky at the little town of Canton. At this town Quantrell rode into a blacksmith shop to have a shoe tightened on his horse and when he attempted to raise the horse's hind foot, it jerked his foot away from the smith and in some unaccountable way, severed the tendon just below the hock joint, making him entirely useless. Quantrell was terribly worried, said he had lost his luck and now that his horse had been crippled, we could take care of ourselves and he would stay there. I then suggested to George Wigginton and Tom Harris that we go on and catch up with Uncle Bob and join his company, and just as we mounted to start, Quantrell called to us, saying he had another horse and would go on and stay with us and we would go through to Virginia.

The day after we left Canton, we met a command of about 800 Federals and stopped and talked and joked with them. We then went to Greenville in Muhlenburg County. We found another command of Federals there. We stopped there, put our horses in the livery stable and invited the Federal commander to go with us to the hotel for dinner, paying the hotel and livery bill with government scrip signed, "Colonel Clark of Colorado!"

When we left this town several of the Federals accompanied us part of the way. Among our escort was a man who was organizing a negro company, styling himself "Captain," and during our ride, continued to boast about what he and his negro company would do to the Southern people. After escorting us a short way, our companions dropped back, except the captain, who went with us a few miles farther, when we left him.

On the next afternoon, we discovered a trail of Federal soldiers and followed them until sundown, where we found them in a house. They had seen us coming and all escaped except six, who remained in the house and opened fire on us. Jim Little and I dismounted and slipping up towards the house, were in a corner of the fence, trying to get a shot at them, when one of them shot Jim through the thigh shattering the bone. As he fell to the ground he said, "John, I am shot; my leg is shattered." Four of us boys placed him in a blanket and carried him across the hill, the Federals shooting at us all the time, and one of the bullets tore the heel off my boot. I was mad and desperate and reaching the yard gate, started towards the house, when Quantrell yelled to me, "John, you damned fool, come back from there." He then ordered the house to be set afire, when the Federals yelled, "We will surrender if you will treat us as prisoners." They then surrendered and were paroled. We brought Jim Little back and left him in the house, the Federals promising to take good care of him. We all went in and told Jim goodbye and left him and learned afterward that he died from his wound.

We then rode all night long and the next morning, after sun up, we stopped at a house for breakfast, where there was an old gentleman, his wife, two daughters and two young men, whom we afterwards learned were Confederate soldiers. While we were eating breakfast, the young ladies continued to ply questions to us, trying to discover who we really were, seeming to know that although we were wearing Federal uniforms we were Confederates.. After breakfast, when we had mounted, the young ladies came out to the fence, and, as we told them good-bye one of them remarked, "Gentlemen, from your manners, we take you to be Southern men, and while I do not know who you are, if you are Southern soldiers. I wish you all the happiness and success that could possibly come to anyone, but if you are Federals, my heartfelt wish is that you all will be in hell before night." Our boys could stand it no longer, and immediately began to cheer. Quantrell, in a very stern mannner, commanded "Silence in ranks; forward, gallop," but taking off his hat, bade the ladies goodbye.

The next day we met two gentlemen, and Will Bassham, engaging in conversation with them found that one of them was of the same name and related to him and that they were both Southern men. Will left us and accompanied his relative home and never

JOHN McCORKLE AND T. B. HARRIS
Taken at Lexington, Missouri, fall, 1864.

138b

joined us again, and we afterwards heard that he had been killed in that county.

On the next day, at the edge of a little village, where there were some Federals stationed, we met five government wagons and while we were talking to the drivers of the wagons, we were fired on by the soldiers from the town, which we returned and rode on, leaving the town to our left, but the Federals did not follow us. About twelve o'clock the next day, having stopped to feed our horses at a horse shed where there were thirty or forty head of horses, some of the boys decided to trade horses, leaving their own horses and taking some out of the shed. Before we got to the town of Houstonville, the owner of the horses caught up with us and remonstrated with us, demanding the return of the horses. Quantrell told him that the boys needed the horses worse than he did and that he had better return to his farm and say nothing about it.

In Houstonville, the boys found three or four fine horses in a livery stable that belonged to a Federal lieutenant and, as we started to leave the town, Allen Palmer mounted a very fine mare that belonged to this lieutenant. The lieutenant rushed up, caught the mare by the bridle, remarking that if she went out of that stable she would go over his dead body, to which Allen replied, "That is a damned easy job," and shot him, and we rode on out of town. We went from there to Danville.

The news that Allen had shot the lieutenant had reached Danville before we did and, as we entered the town, a company of Federals came out to meet us, but after some talk with Colonel Quantrell, they returned to the town and we followed them. When we had reached the courthouse square, Quantrell drew up in line and gave the order to dismount, which we understood to mean, Quantrell having previously told us, to dash forward and compel every soldier and man in the town to fall in line. We immediately made a rush, telling them all to fall in and face us. Quantrell was sitting on his horse in front of a store, when the lieutenant rushed out with a rifle in his hand and, leveling it at Quantrell, said, "I want to see your papers." The Colonel replied, "My orderly has my commission and papers." The colonel then ordered John Barker to advance with them. The lieutenant turned to receive the papers from John, when the colonel suddenly drew his revolver and, leveling it on the lieutenant, said, "Here are my papers; now drop that gun," when the lieutenant's mother rushed up to the colonel and said, "He is my boy; for my sake do not kill him." Quantrell replied, "Well, madam, for your sake I will not. Take him and make him behave himself, but if he bothers me any more, I may kill him." Turning in his saddle, he told the soldiers and the men to all go home and let him alone, that he intended to hurt no one. We then put spurs to our horses, and turning to the southwest, left Harrodsburg to our right. Night was then coming on and we divided into squads to get our suppers. John Barker and eleven men stopped at one house; I, in command of seven men, stopped at another house and Quantrell and the remainder went to the next house. While we were eating our supper, I heard firing at the house where Barker had stopped. Chad Renick, who was with me, rushed out and jumping on his horse, started toward the house and I followed him. Just as he reached the top of the hill, I heard Chad exclaim, "Quit firing down there," and then I met his horse coming back without a rider. Catching his horse by the bridle, I advanced a few yards farther and turned and rode back, ordering my boys to mount, intending to go on where Quantrell was.

When we reached the house, we found Quantrell had left, having discovered a company of Federals coming across a field. A lady ran out of the house and asking us if we were Confederates, went back into the house and brought us out some fried chicken and biscuit, telling the direction Quantrell had taken.

We afterwards learned that while John Barker and his men were at supper the Federals had surrounded the house and, as the boys started out, fired on them, killing John Barker, Henry Noland, and Foss Key and had killed Chad Renick as he came over the hill before me and that they had captured Dick Glasscock, Jim Younger, Bill Gaugh, Vess Aker, Jack Graham, Dick Burns, George Robinson, Tom Evans and Andy McGuire. These last nine named were taken to Lexington and placed in jails and on three different occasions were taken out into the jail yard to be hung, but each time the boys would come out of the jail cheering for Jeff Davis and daring them to hang them, telling them their deaths would be avenged.

In April, eight of them were taken to Louisville and placed in prison, where afterwards, with the assistance of some of the citizens, they escaped. Tom Evans was kept in jail at Lexington, the Federals thinking he had killed the Lieutenant at Houstonville, but after the war, he was released.

After the lady had given us the fired chicken, we found Colonel Quantrell with his squad drawn up in line of battle. I asked him what to do about the other boys. He said he did not know what to do, that he was afraid none of us could get back there without being killed, but if I felt like risking it, to go ahead. I told him that if any of the other boys would go with me. I would try it. Payne Jones and Allen Palmer rode out of line and said they would go with me. I then changed horses, mounting Chad Renick's horse. We started through the fields, letting down the fences and leaving them down so that we could retreat. When we had reached the cross road, I told the boys that I would stay there and keep a look-out and for them to go towards the house. They had scarcely gotten a hundred yards from me when I discovered a company of Federals coming between us and Colonel Quantrell. I called to the boys to stop but they could not hear me. I put spurs to my horse and caught up with them. We immediately turned and, riding at a gallop, came in front of the company of Federals. I asked who they were and they replied Bridgewater's men and asked who we were. I replied, "Clark's men" and was answered with a volley. We returned the fire and dashed down the hill and across a branch, they following us, shooting and yelling.

At this time, my horse begun to act as if he had never been under fire before and was trying his best to throw me and when we had reached one of the gaps in the fence, he refused to go through it, but kept on down through the woods. I could not stop him nor turn him. Just then Payne Jones yelled to me, "Hell fire, John, what are you doing? Look in front of you," and when I raised my head, I saw a company of Federals not sixty yards away, formed in line. I pulled all the strength I had on one bridle rein and, turning his head toward a fence, buried my spurs in his side. He did not jump, but went through the fence, scattering the rails in all directions. Just then the Federals opened fire and killed Jones' horse. Jones tried to get behind me, but my horse was acting so badly he could not. I opened fire then, while he got behind Palmer. Riding up by the side of Palmer's horse, I told Jones to get on behind me, as I had the stronger horse and without stopping our horses, he swung from Palmer's horse to mine. We then, in a few minutes, reached Quantrell and the Federals quit following us.

After riding seven or eight miles, we came to a large corn-pen at the corner of a field and pasture, where we stayed all night. The next morning, we stopped at a farmer's house and he told us that he knew of no Federals nearer than Harrodsburg, but that over in Nelson County, he said that there was a noted character by the name of Sue Munday, who was guerrilla. After eating breakfast here, we started for Nelson County, riding all day until three or four o'clock in the afternoon, and, as we were entering a lane, which was fenced on either side with a famous Kentucky post and rail fence, we discovered a company of Federals about a quarter of a mile distant, coming in our direction. Quantrell ordered me to go ahead and tear the fence down, but I could do nothing with it. He then told me to go ahead until I found a gate or a pair of bars. In the meantime, the Federals had got out into the road in our rear. Just as I reached the town of Mayfield, I found a gate leading into a pasture. Quantrell and the men riding up, he said, "Rush, boys, those fellows are coming like the devil." He and the command rushed through and I remained to shut the gate, the Federals firing three or four shots at me. We went over a hill and formed in line of battle, the Federals following us and were right on us before they discovered us. We charged them and they wheeled and went back through the gate and did not attempt to follow us any further, as they passed a house they asked an old negro who we were, and he told them, that we were strangers to him, "but my advice, marster, would be, not to follow them men any further, because, befo' God, they had more pistols on them than any men he had ever seen befo'."

When we had proceeded a short distance in the pasture I saw a man riding down the creek and Quantrell told me to go see what he wanted. I rode up behind him and when I spoke to him he turned and saw the command and became very much excited. I told him not to be excited, that we were all

Southern men and were from Missouri. He then told me that in the town of Mayfield, there were two Southern families, one by the name of Saunders and a widow, by the name of Cooper. I knew both of these families, as they had formerly lived in Jackson County, Missouri, and had been forced to leave there under Order No. 11. He then told me his name was Russell, and taking him back to the command, I introduced him to Colonel Quantrell and he asked us to go over to his house and stay all night with him. During all this time Mr. Russell seemed to doubt who we were, and Quantrell suggested that he take two or three of the boys, accompanied by Mr. Russell and go over into town and see these Missouri families. After the visit to the town, Mr. Russell was thoroughly satisfied that we were Southerners.

We stayed around in Nelson County some time, sleeping in the woods at night and enjoying Kentucky hospitality. Near where we were, there was a large still-house, owned by an old gentleman by the name of Jim Dawns. We called on him one morning and he gave us a genuine Kentucky welcome, bringing out a water-bucket of his best but none of us became intoxicated and, at his earnest solicitation, we spent the day with him.

Late that afternoon, John Hunter, a resident of Spencer County, invited George Wigginton, John Barnhill, Will Parker and me to go across Salt River into Spencer County and get acquainted with some of the Southern people over there. There we became acquainted with two families by the name of Wigginton, who were related to George and met Mr.

Aaron Thurman, who had two beautiful daughters, Miss Jennie and Miss Dollie and I must confess that I was very much impressed with Miss Jennie and afterwards made frequent visits to call on her.

One day George Wigginton, Will Parker, John Hunter and I were in the woods north of Mr. Thurman's house when a body of Federal soldiers came from Taylorsville looking for us. Miss Jennie saw them coming and going over to a neighbor's house, whose name was John Stilwell, she and Mrs. Stilwell came to the woods and told us they were coming. We mounted our horses and riding to the edge of the woods, amused ourselves watching the Federals circling around the woods looking for us. They circled the woods three times, but never entered it and, finally, giving up the hunt, they returned to Taylorville and we went up to one of the Wigginton's for supper.

About this time there was in this country a certain man styling himself Major Metz, who claimed to be a Southern soldier, but who was in reality, a deserter from the Union Army and for whose arrest the Federal authorities at Louisville had offered a reward of $500.

Metz had married a woman by the name of Walker, who bore a very unsavory reputation and was living with her father near Mr. Thurman's. There had been a number of citizens and also a number of country stores in this neighborhood recently robbed. When we reached Wigginton's place that evening, we were told that the night before two men had gone to the home of a very old man by the name of Duncan, and finding no one at home but the old man and his wife, had demanded of Duncan his money and upon his telling them that he had no money there, having sent all his money to Louisville, they began to abuse him, placing his finger-nails under the ramrods of their pistols and mashing them off. They left him thus mutilated, taking with them $30 in money that he had. When they started to leave Duncan, they told him that they were Missourians and if he ever told who they were they would return and kill both him and his wife. When Mr. Wigginton told me this, I told him we would investigate it, that we neither robbed nor mistreated citizens and asked him to go over to Duncan's house and try to find out who they were, but Mr. Duncan refused to disclose their identity.

I then went down to see Mr. Duncan and told him that we were Missourians and that we never mistreated anyone, and that our commander, Colonel Quantrell, would not countenance such acts, and that we did not propose to have the blame laid on us and I wanted him to tell me who they were. He told me he knew who they were, but was afraid to tell, that they would come and kill him. I told him that if he would tell me who they were, I would assure him that they would never bother him again, and he finally told me that it was Major Metz and another man.

I at once went back into Nelson County and told Quantrell. He said, "Well, why didn't you go get him? Go back and catch them and make short work of them. We do not rob people and I swear no man can accuse us of such hellish acts as this and live." I immediately returned and for several days tried to catch Major Metz, but he escaped me, and one day a citizen of that county came to me and told me that he would capture Metz and his companion for $10. I told him I would give them $10 apiece to bring them to me. The next morning he returned bringing Major Metz with him. I gave him the $10 and took the Major in charge. After taking the latter's pistol away from him, he inquired what I wanted with him and I told him, "We want you for robbing old man Duncan and pinching his fingers off and treating him so brutally, then trying to lay your devilish conduct on us Missourians, and I am going to kill you for doing it." He commenced to beg and ask me for mercy. I told him that he had had no mercy on defenseless old men and women and that any brute who would treat an old man like he had treated old man Duncan had no right to live. He then asked me to take him near his home before I killed him and, as we reached his father-in-law's gate, old man Walker came running out of the house, calling to us, "Take that damned thief away from here and kill him. I never want him in this yard again. He has done nothing but rob and steal ever since he has been in this county, pretending he was a Southern man, when he is nothing but a damned thieving Yankee, take him away and kill him.' We led the Major into the woods and he was soon deprived of all desire to steal and rob and had abused and mistreated his last man. Old man Walker called us back to the house, saying, "I want you men to go into the room that

COLONEL WILLIAM QUANTRELL.

148b

Metz has used to hide his plunder in. He has been doing nothing but robbing people in this country for the last year and I was too old and feeble to prevent it and he threatened to kill me if I told." We went into the room and found a large box filled with drygoods, boots and shoes and all kinds of articles scattered around the room.

We returned and I reported to Colonel Quantrell what we had done with Metz and, after staying with him a few days, John Barnhill and I returned to Mr. Thurman's in Spencer County. There I met a Captain Stone, who was recruiting for the Confederates. When Captain Stone had secured a number of recruits, they would be turned over to a Colonel Jesse, who would take them back to Virginia.

A few days after we had returned, Miss Jennie Thurman prepared a fine dinner for us and Captain Stone was invited to join us. After dinner, we went back into Nelson County and Colonel Quantrell led us on a little trip up between Louisville and Taylorsville, and just before reaching Taylorsville, we saw a negro regiment marching in the direction of that town. We rode into the woods and would ride up to the edge of the timber, fire into them, and dash back into the woods. We kept this up until they had reached the town of Taylorsville. There we let them alone and started toward Salt River. Just before we had reached Salt River, a man met us and handed Colonel Quantrell a paper, telling him to read it to us. It was an account of the assassination of Abraham Lincoln. Before the Colonel had finished reading it, we all began to cheer and, breaking ranks, we all started at a gallop and never stopped until we had reached Jim Dawns' still house, where we stayed for a day or two.

We then separated and remained in hiding for several days, when we returned to Nelson County and found Colonel Quantrell. We there held a conference, having just heard that General Lee had surrendered and, knowing the war was over, we decided to separate and make the best terms of surrender we could. Quantrell then told us that before we separated, he had another act to perform, that he had just been told that a man, claiming to be a Missourian and one of our men, had robbed an old citizen by the name of Jones, and that the description given of the robber fitted one of our men, telling me the name of the man. He said he was going to take the man described to old man Jones and if the old man identified him he would have him killed, that he never had permitted, nor never would permit any of his men to commit robbery. I then told Quantrell that as the man he suspicioned had been with me in a number of close places and considered him a brave soldier, that I would not go with him on such a mission. He told me all right and to meet him in a day or two at Mrs. Cooper's and, turning, he rode away. This was the last time I ever saw Quantrell. Tom Harris, George Wigginton and John Barnhill stayed with me and we went back to Thurman's house. After Colonel Quantrell left us, he started to go to Jones' house and when he and his men reached the pike leading from Taylorsville to Bloomfield, a very haevy rain came up and they turned off of the pike and went into Dr. Wakefield's barn. Being very tried, he laid down on a pile of hay to rest. The boys began to romp and throw cobs at each other and four or five of them were pelting John Ross with cobs and he ran out of the barn door into the lot, when he saw a compan yof Federals coming through the lot gate. This company was under the command of Captain Mead. John ran back to the door and yelled, "Great God, boys, the Federals are right on us." Quantrell sprang up and said, "Mount, about face and charge." He ran to his horse and as he started to mount him, his stirrup leather broke, throwing him across his saddle and, before he could regain his position, his horse dashed out of the door, following the other horses, and just as his horse entered the lot with him, a Federal shot him in the back, the bullet ranging up and forward. His horse ran with him into a pasture. Quantrell still trying to regain his seat and, as the horse made a turn, he fell to the ground on his back and a Federal rode by him, shooting at him when he exclaimed, "It is useless to shoot me any more; I am now a dying man." The Federals carried him into Dr. Wakefield's house, where his wounds were dressed and the Federals left him there that night. After the Federals left him, Frank James, John Ross, Bill Hulse and Payne Jones went to see him and wanted to take him away and hide him in the woods, but he declined to go, saying, "Boys, it is impossible for me to get well, the war is over and I am in reality a dying man, so let me alone. Goodbye," and the boys turned and left him. In a few days, the Federals came with an ambulance and took him to Louisville, placing him in a hospital. He remained in the hospital at Louisville for several weeks, when a Catholic priest, who had been visiting him, telling the authorities that he was bound to die, prevailed upon them to let him be removed to a Catholic hospital, where on the seventh day of June, 1865, the spirit of one of the truest, bravest men that ever lived passed from earth to appear before his maker and render an account for the deeds done here.

There has been in late years a number of sensational articles appearing in the public press, claiming that Quantrell was not dead and at various times some one, to gain notoriety, has published a statement that Quantrell was still alive, but I know that he died at Louisville, Kentucky. I know that just before his death, he gave the priest an order to Mrs. Cooper for the money he had left with her. These facts I have from a reliable authority, Miss Eliza Sanders, who was familiar with all of these facts, and who wrote them to me after the war. In 1872, Miss Mary Beverley, of Howard County, Missouri, who afterwards married Bill Greenwood, was in Louisville, Kentucky, hunted us his grave, which she found from the records kept by the sexton of the Catholic graveyard and had it re-sodded.

It will be remembered that four of us did not go with Quantrell on his last trip, but waited for him near Mrs. Cooper's and having waited in vain a day and night, I rode out on the pike to see if I could hear anything of him and just as I came in sight of Dr. Wakefield's house, I met Mr. Russell and asked him if he knew anything of our boys. He said, "Your captain was shot day before yesterday and is mortally wounded," and turning towards Dr. Wakefield's house, he pointed to a lot of men in front of the house and said, "There are the Federal soldiers now with an ambulance taking your colonel to Louisville.

George Wigginton and I then went back into Spencer County to Mr. Thurman's and remained for several days, where we again met Captain Stone and he told us that he was going to Newcastle to surrender and that we had better go and surrender as new recruits with him. We consulted with Mr. Thurman and some other friends and they decided that, as Quantrell's command was not recognized in Kentucky as regular Confederate soldiers, it would probably be better for us to surrender with Captain Stone. We then bade our Kentucky friends good-bye and I must confess that it was a sad parting between Miss Jennie Thurman and myself. I had with me at that time the fine Colt's revolvers, with their scabbards and belt that I had taken from the trunk of the Federal officer at Baxter Springs. I presented these to Miss Jennie, with my compliments, telling her that I might some day return and claim them, but I have never seen any of the Thurman family since.

We went with Captain Stone, riding at night, until we came to the town of Newcastle, Kentucky, and about four o'clock in the morning, we stopped at the house of a distinguished citizen of that country, Mr. Joseph Prior, who was a first cousin of the illustirous jurist, Judge Prior, of the Kentucky Court of

Appeals and was also the father of William Prior, who afterwards moved to Missouri and was for four years Clerk of the County Court of Howard County. Mr. Prior came to the door and invited us in and, after telling us to remain at his house and he would go to Newcastle, see the Federal authorities and arrange to have us paroled. He returned from Newcastle with a Federal colonel and a lieutenant colonel, who treated us very nicely and stayed until after dinner, talking with us about the war and on other topics, and when they were ready to leave, they took our arms and horses and paroled us and administered to us the oath of allegiance to the Federal government, which we have both kept ever since.

After the Federals left us, we decided it was better for us to leave at once and Mr. Prior had two of his horses saddled and, telling one of his boys to ride behind us, he started us to Port Royal, giving us a letter of introduction to a friend of his there. When we reached the house of this friend of his, we handed him the letter and he gave us a hearty welcome, but told us that the Owen County militia might be on that side of the river and we had better go into the woods and stay until night, when we could return to his house as the militia always returned to Owen County at night. After dark, we returned to his house and retired. This was the first time I had slept all night in a house in three years.

In the morning, he advised us to return to the brush and stay until he could make arrangements for a boat to take us down the river. When we saw a boat coming down the river, he took us to the shore and made arrangements for our transportation and we went to Madison, Indiana, where we stayed all night and from there, we went to Indianapolis and to Terre Haute, then to Evansville, where we stayed several days and from Evansville, we went by river to Paducah, Kentucky, and to our uncle, Colonel Robert Fristoe. There I went to work on the farm of a Mr. Cobb and George Wigginton went to work for uncle Robert Fristoe.

After we had been there for about a month, we received a letter from my cousin, Mollie Wigginton, in which she told us that they were still holding Tom Evans at Lexington, Kentucky, charging him with having shot and killed the lieutenant at Houstonville, and as we both knew that Tom did not shoot the lieutenant, but that Allen Palmer was the one that killed him, for us to go before some Notary Public and make an affidavit to these facts and send them to Lexington and she also stated in the letter that they all wanted us to come home. George and I went to Mayfield, Kentucky, and made the affidavit as suggested and forwarded it to Lexington.

At this time, we were both homesick and longing for old Missouri and, in a few days, we started home. Going to Paducah, Kentucky, we took a steam boat on the Ohio River and went to Cairo, taking another boat and going from there to St. Louis. From St. Louis we went to Jefferson City on the Missouri Pacific Railroad, and after staying there a day or two, we went by boat to Glasgow, in Howard County. I then went to the home of my uncle, John Fristoe, who lived north of Glasgow, he had been a refugee from Jackson County. I stayed in this vicinity for several years, working on farm and, in November, 1867, I was married and have lived in Howard County, Missouri ever since.

It will be remembered that George Wigginton and I were not present at the fight at the barn when Colonel Quantrell was wounded, he and I, with our two companions later surrendering at Winchester, Kentucky, and the first account I had of the surrender of the remainder of the command was given me after the war by Frank James. He told me that, after Quantrell was removed to Louisville, they appointed another commander, and, in a few days, he went into Bardstown, Kentucky, and saw Captain Mead, who was a true soldier and a brave man, and agreed on terms of surrender. They then reported to Captain Mead, who met them near Bardstown, with a few of his men, and he told them to keep their arms and horses and remain with him until he could hear from General Palmer, who was in command at Louisville.

While waiting to hear from General Palmer, it was reported to Captain Mead that two men had outraged a woman living in the country. Captain Mead tried for several days to apprehend them, but failed. Frank James then told him that he could take six of his men and capture these two fiends. Mead told him to go ahead and he left with five other men and, in a few days, captured them and, taking them to the woman, who promptly identified them, and, acting under the instructions of Captain Mead, James had them shot. Placing the bodies in a wagon he took them back to Captain Mead, telling him what he had done. Captain Mead congratulated him and thanked him for his actions in this matter and assured him that he would notify General Palmer fully in regard to it, and, in a few days, General Palmer issued an order for the boys to be paroled and that they be permitted to keep their arms and horses and, after taking the oath of allegiance to the Federal government, allowed them to go in peace to their homes.

This is a true story of my life during the war. Nearly all the men who fought and suffered with me are dead. There are only a few of us left and ere long the last Missouri guerilla will be only a memory. I realize that but a few years at least remain for me. My record since the war is known to my neighbors and friends and, while, in my declining years, these scenes come up to me as horrible dreams, I feel thankful that my life has been spared this long and hope that my enemies will forgive me for any worng act of mine, as I know my Maker has. This book has been written at my dictation by my young friend and written in the spirit expressed in the language of Abraham Lincoln, "with malice toward none and with charity to all."

Printed in Great Britain
by Amazon